The Beaded Edge

Inspired Designs for Crocheted Edgings and Trims

Midori Nishida & CRK design

design-1
design-6
design-4
design-7
design-2
design-3
design-5

The Beaded Edge:
Inspired Designs for Crocheted Edgings and Trims
by Midori Nishida & CRK design

First designed and published in Japan as "Edging with Beads by Crochet and
Needle Vol. 1" in 2009
by Graphic-sha Publishing Co., Ltd.
1-14-17 Kudan-kita, Chiyoda-ku,
Tokyo 102-0073 Japan

© 2009 Midori Nishida
© 2009 CRK design
© 2009 Graphic-sha Publishing Co., Ltd.

English edition published in 2010
by Interweave Press LLC

First published in the United States of America by
Interweave Press
201 East Fourth Street
Loveland, CO 80537-5655
interweave.com

ISBN-13: 978-1-59668-300-6

10 9 8 7 6 5 4 3 2 1

Planning, production and editing: Midori Nishida & CRK design
                                   (Chiaki Kitaya, Kaoru Emoto, Kuma Imamura,
                                   Kumiko Yajima, Noriko Yoshiue, Yasuko Endo)
Motif design: Midori Nishida
Piece design and production: Midori Nishida & CRK design
Collaborators: Kanji Ishimoto, Chieko Ishimoto
Photography: Yoshiharu Ohtaki (studio seek)
Procedure photography: Nobuei Araki (studio seek)
Styling: Tomomi Enai
Model: Sylvia
Hair and makeup: Yuka Murakami, Yumi Hareyama
Book design and illustration: CRK design

English edition layout: Shinichi Ishioka
English translation: Sean Gaston, Yuko Watda, Nozomi Wakui,
                                   Takako Otomo
Project management: Kumiko Sakamoto
                                   (Graphic-sha Publishing Co., Ltd.)

Printed and bound in China

design-10
design-13
design-16
design-14
design-11
design-17
design-15
design-18

Contents

Edging with Beads using a Crochet Hook

4	design-1	**Window -Box**
6	design-2	**Orchard**
8	design-3	**Refreshing Breeze**
10	design-4	**Dewdrops in the Meadow**
12	design-5	**Fluttering Butterflies**
14	design-6	**Church Bells**
16	design-7	**Dainty Berries**
18	design-8	**Soap Bubbles**
20	design-9	**Enchanting Wild Roses**
22	design-10	**A Floral Hedge**
24	design-11	**A Garden of Pansies**
26	design-12	**Lace Flowers**
28	design-13	**A Sun-dazzled Footpath**
30	design-14	**Sparkling Fringe**

Edging with Beads using a Beading Needle

32	design-15	**Triangular Hat**
34	design-16	**Stars Twinkling over Snow**
36	design-17	**Juicy Grapes**
38	design-18	**Tiny Hot Peppers**

Remake Idea Collection

40	SCARF	**Beaded Edging for a scarf**
42	WEDDING	**Beaded Edging for wedding items**
44	NOËL	**Beaded Edging for Christmas items**
46	FOLKLORE	**Beaded Edging for Folkloric Items**
48	FOLKLORE	**Babushka**
49	SUMMER	**A Linen Parasol**
50	SUMMER	**Beaded Edging for Summer**
52	CRAFT ZAKKA	**Beaded Edging for Home Décor and Gifts**

54	**Beautiful Turkish Edgings**
58	**Materials & Tools**
60	**Recipe Note**
87	**ABCs of Edging with Beads**

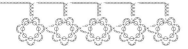

design-1
Window-Box

Instructions: see page 60

Designed by Midori Nishida Created by Kayomi Yokoyama

Beaded edging for a spring colored scarf

Fashion together a look of pretty bead flowers on a base crocheted with bugle beads. Highlight a spring blossom colored silk scarf gently swinging in the breeze with this bead edging.

design-2
Orchard

Instructions: see page 65

Designed by Midori Nishida Created by Kayomi Yokoyama

Beaded edging for a T-shirt

Crocheted with round beads in two colors, this motif, with the look of mouthwateringly ripe fruit, adds a little panache to the thick T-shirt fabric. Embellish the edges of both sleeves with the same motif to spice it up even more.

design-3

Refreshing Breeze

Instructions: see page 66

Designed and Created by Midori Nishida

Beaded edging for a blouse

Each of these beautifully patterned fans is accentuated with colored beads in the center. This versatile motif crocheted with white yarn and elegant gold beads will complement a variety of outfits, as the color of the four central beads can be swapped to mix and match your wardrobe. I brightened up a white cotton blouse with this motif to lend it a simple-yet-elegant feel.

design-4

Dewdrops in the Meadow

Instructions: see page 67

Designed by Midori Nishida   Created by MEU

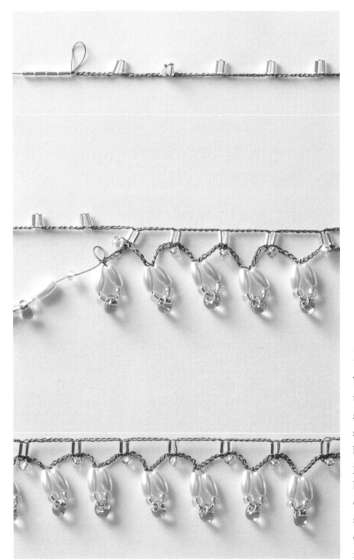

Beaded edging for a skirt

This piece was fashioned together with an eclectic assortment of beads, from silver bugle beads, light-blue round beads, pearl jujube-shaped beads to blue magatama beads. This captivating skirt edging sparkles gloriously as it catches the light with every movement.

design-5
Fluttering Butterflies

Instructions: see page **68**

Designed and Created by Midori Nishida

Summery hat decoration

Why not work some linen yarn in to create a summery look? Invest in some fine linen yarn from your neighborhood leather craft shop, and you will be delighted to discover that even small round beads can be easily slid onto your chosen material. Crochet in alternate colors to breathe your butterflies to life. Wound gently round a raffia straw hat, it makes a perfect alternative to a ribbon.

Church Bells

Instructions: see page 69

Designed by Midori Nishida Created by Kuma Imamura

Lariat with linen yarn

Based on a Turkish motif called 'the broom,' this lariat was put together using brightly colored round beads and fine linen yarn. The idea was to create an accessory, to match a folkloric-style tunic. Casually draping it about your neck adds a burst of exciting colors.

Dainty Berries

Instructions: see page **70**

Designed and Created by Midori Nishida

Beaded edging for a camisole

The "Mulberry" is a popular berry motif often crocheted in Turkey. Simply replacing the green beads on the tip with red transforms it into a "strawberry." Imagining that vivid red berries might appear a bit too cutesy for a lovely lace-trimmed camisole, I instead selected wine-colored beads to present a darker tone. The moss green chain adds the perfect contrast to the expressive color of the berries.

Soap Bubbles

Instructions: see page 71

Design and Created by Midori Nishida

Edging jean pocket flaps

A common motif known as 'the bird's eye' in Turkey, many variations can be created by simply adjusting the number of beads. You can quickly progress by adding one bubble after another and these pocket flaps can be edged in a jiff. As you can see, edging also looks great on jeans.

Enchanting Wild Roses

Instructions: see page 62

Designed by Midori Nishida Created by MEU

Beaded edging for a sweater

At first, fashion some six-bead petals, following this by adding a new layer of five-bead petals with additional beads in the center to create a sense of depth and dimension. Even a single rose can add a classy touch and makes it well worth the added effort. Evenly spacing some of these delightful roses on a plain but high quality wool sweater really livens it up

design-10
A Floral Hedge

Instructions: see page 72

Designed by Midori Nishida Created by Yurie Yura

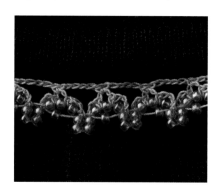

Beaded edging for an ensemble

This bright red edging is reminiscent of a hedge of wild azaleas. A breeze to make, once you start crocheting away, you'll find yourself finishing the whole length in no time. Embellishing a black ensemble with this motif adds a unique and personal touch to it.

design-11
A Garden of Pansies

Instructions: see page 73

Designed by Midori Nishida Created by Kayomi Yokoyama

**Beaded edging for
a wool camisole**

This darling edging was inspired by garden pansies bursting into bloom. I trimmed the neckline of a soft wool camisole with round bead flowers, and edged the hem with another small bouquet composed of smaller round beads. Since only one color per row is used, you'll have the beads in the right order in no time. Explore a variety of different color combos until you find something that matches your taste.

Lace Flowers

Instructions: see page **74**

Designed by Midori Nishida Created by Yurie Yura

Beaded edging for a stole

Adding red beads can accentuate an otherwise gold motif. This piece combines thick lace yarn with round beads to smoothly blend into the soft fabric of the stole. With lace flowers bordering its fringeless edges, it emanates a captivating aura anyway you wear it.

A Sun-dazzled Footpath

Instructions: see page 75

Designed and Created by Midori Nishida

Beaded edging for a coat

This piece is reminiscent of a sunny path winding its way through the forest, offering you a leisurely expedition for picking wild plants and flowers. It's surprisingly easy to make, as you can quickly progress through by simply twisting it into loops. Team up round beads with smaller round beads and combine it with lace yarn. This beaded braid naturally curves inward, and pleasantly harmonizes with the rounded collar of the coat.

design-14
Sparkling Fringe

Instructions: see page **76**

Designed and Created by Midori Nishida Created by Yasuko Endo

Beaded edging for a petite bag

This beaded fringe is a simple variation on the "A Sun-dazzled Footpath" braid (p.28). Adding sparkling fringes to the hem will turn this classic-looking bag into a standout at any party. Add a moderate amount of glittering three-cut gold beads into the mix for a tasteful accent.

design-15
Triangular Hat

Instructions: see page 77

Designed by Midori Nishida Created by Yuko Ueki

Beaded edging for a poncho

Form a triangular hat with 9mm-long bugle beads and add a single spangle to the top. Take the beads with a threaded needle, and attach the hats to the chain stitch base one by one. I edged a simple red poncho with this motif as an alternative to fringes. These charming little hats swing and sway with your every move.

design-16

Stars Twinkling over Snow

Instructions: see page **78**

Designed by Midori Nishida Created by Yuko Ueki

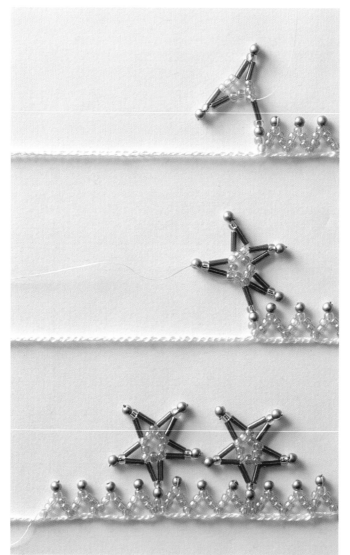

Beaded edging for a bag

If you know how to draw a star with one stroke, then this motif will be quite straightforward. Place beads in the right order with a threaded needle, and attach one star after another to the chain stitch base. I edged a fluffy wool bag and a matching phone case with these beautiful twinkly stars.

Juicy Grapes

Instructions: see page **79**

Designed and Created by Midori Nishida

A wine-colored choker

This motif was made using a technique in which beads are woven together with a needle and beading thread to create delicate beaded objects. Subtly sparkling antique beads garnishing the evenly spaced grapes lend a classic air to this piece. Add a layer of double crochet to the chain stitch base and this choker will make a chic addition to any black or wine-colored outfit.

Tips: The "bead stitch," also known as off-loom beading, is a beading technique for weaving beads using a needle and without a loom. This is a centuries-old technique employed in various parts of the world, ideal for making beaded accessories.

design-18

Tiny Hot Peppers

Instructions: see page **80**

Designed by Midori Nishida Created by Kumiko Yajima

Beaded edging for kitchen items

Slip green beads onto the beading thread with a needle as you work through. Flatten the hot pepper piece utilizing the off-loom beading technique, and later roll it into a round shape. I lavishly embellished some kitchen cloths with these cute little peppers. Yellow and green peppers can be interspersed with red ones.

SCARF
Beaded Edging for a Scarf

Instructions: see page 81

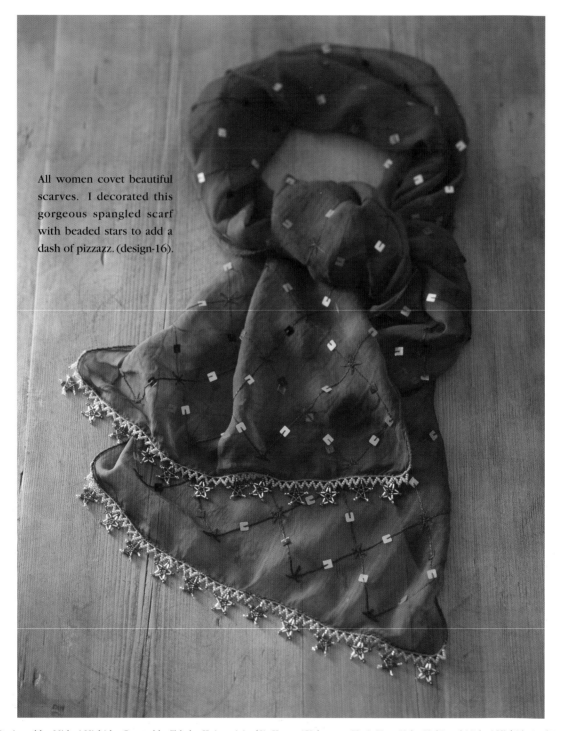

All women covet beautiful scarves. I decorated this gorgeous spangled scarf with beaded stars to add a dash of pizzazz. (design-16).

Designed by Midori Nishida Created by Takako Koizumi (p.40), Kayomi Yokoyama, Yurie Yura, Yuko Ueki and Midori Nishida (p.41)

(P. 41, from top to bottom: design-7, design-10, design-12, design-11, design-8, design-1, design-15, see photo for actual bead colors)

Beaded Edging for Wedding Items

Instructions: see page 81

Adorn yourself with a veil embellished with hand-made edging at the moment you pledge your eternal love, the happiest in your life. The gently swaying something-blue beaded edging is about 6.3 meters (248 inches) in length and brings a touch of delicate elegance to the veil (design-10).

Designed by Midori Nishida Created by Yurie Yura, Yasuko Endo and Midori Nishida

Trim the ring pillow with round beads and pearl beads of matching color (design-2). The beaded rose adds to the delicate charm of this pillow (design-9).

A matching bridal pouch to carry your cherished items and wedding day necessities (design -12).

NOËL
Beaded Edging for Christmas Items

Instructions: see page 82

Here's hoping Santa has lots of gifts and goodies under the tree for me. I decked my Christmas boots with prettily crocheted beaded edgings. (design-10, 3)

Designed by Midori Nishida Created by Takako Koizumi and Noriko Yoshiue

Dress up the linen garlands with sparkling beads and spangles to lend them a Christmassy touch. (design-15, 16)

Adorable felt ornaments. The snowman and little bird are looking pleased as Christmas punch with dainty bead necklaces entwined about their necks. (design-15, 16)

FOLKLORE
Beaded Edging for Folkloric Items

Instructions: see page 83, 84

I used a wood bead edging to trim a plain knit cap in my favorite colors. If formed long enough, it can be twisted and pinned over the ears to form corsages, with the ends hanging free.

(design-2)

Designed by Midori Nishida Created by Kuma Imamura and Yasuko Endo

These plump berries crocheted with wood beads are perfect for dressing up your Western boots and lends them a bit of a Native American feel. (design-7 & 10)

Fashion a sufficiently long piece and twist it into small corsages.

Keep yourself toasty and cozy on those crispy and chilly wintery days with a bag and gloves that ooze warmth. Vividly-colored wool yarn was teamed up with wood beads to design these edgings. (design-3 & 12)

FOLKLORE
Babushka

Instructions: see page **86**

This triangular babushka, a variation of the Soap Bubbles motif on page 18, is 39 bubbles wide and 20 bubbles high, with each bubble made up of six beads. Colored beads used at regular intervals form an enigmatic motif. (design-8)

Designed and Created by Midori Nishida

SUMMER
A Linen Parasol

Instructions: see page 84

Designed by Midori Nishida Created by Kayomi Yokoyama

Grab people's attention with this parasol sparkling brilliantly away under the summer sun. This motif, though a cinch to put together, appears a bit complicated because of how light flickers and dances in the beads. (design-1)

Glass beads are perfectly matched for summer. These transparent blue beads come across as refreshingly cool and summery. Try your hand at making butterfly glass markers in two colors with matching coasters. (design-5)

SUMMER
Beaded Edging for Summer

Instructions: see page 75, 84

Designed and Created by Midori Nishida
Created by Kayomi Yokoyama and Yasuko Endo

I successfully trimmed a café curtain with the "bell" motif on p.14. You can easily transform the bell into a carnation if you replace the original colors with green and pink. See the photo for actual bead colors. (design-6)

A lariat crocheted with silk lace yarn and round beads in two colors. Fringes fashioned together with spiral bugle beads twirl this way and that in the summer breeze.(design-13)

CRAFT ZAKKA
Beaded Edging for Home Décor and Gifts

Instructions: see page 64, 83, 85

Designed and Created by Midori Nishida
Created by Kumiko Yajima and Noriko Yoshiue

Beaded edgings are not just for fabrics, but can also be attached to home décor items. The beads glisten daintily, reflecting the gently flickering candle light. With charming edgings like these, wouldn't you feel like leaving the candle holders out on the table all day, even during the day?
(design - 14, 17, 8, 8 + 6)

(Box in the top: design-3; and glass jars: design-7, 18. See the photo for actual bead colors.)

When bestowing a gift to that special someone, add a personal touch to the wrapping with hand-made edgings. There's no better way to express your feelings to your loved ones. (Front card: design-9; Two center cards: design -11 & 8; album: design-8 &16; box with 3 motifs: design -11, 8 & 10; and the small box with grape motif: design-17)

53

Beautiful Turkish Edgings

Text: Midori Nishida Photo: Yoshiharu Ohtaki Collection: Kanji Ishimoto and Chieko Ishimoto

Decorative edgings are known as "oya" in Turkish. Turkish women embellish their scarves with various types of striking oya edgings. This section highlights various oya edgings made with different types of beads.

Fan

Rose

Cherry

Chamomile

Mulberry

Butterfly

Techniques and motifs handed down from generation to generation

The vast majority of the Turkish population is Muslim. Nowadays, especially in large cities, you rarely catch sight of women swathed from head to toe in the traditional black veil, though you may occasionally run across women sporting headscarves. In rural and provincial Turkey, however, with its deeply-rooted religious traditions and centuries-old customs, you stand a much better chance of encountering local women in scarves. In actuality, wearing a scarf is a must on certain occasions, especially when praying in an Islamic mosque. Many mosques frequented by tourists provide scarves to female visitors so they are able to observe local custom and cover their heads before entering.

These scarves are made from silk or a cotton with a gauze-like texture. Several types of lace edgings to embellish scarves exist: "Iğne oya" is the art of making motifs such as flowers, fruits and geometric patterns by knotting threads with needles. "Tiğ oya", is a motif made with a crochet hook. "Mekik oya" is a form of tatting lace. "Firkete oya" is a hair pin lace, and "Boncuk oya" is made with beads. The most eye-catching of all is "Iğne oya", with a diverse range of intricate and delicate yet gorgeous-looking floral motifs.

Beads can add to the weight of the scarf, so very small or even smaller micro beads are used for certain motifs to minimize weight. Of course very fine threads and needles are required to make oya with such small beads. The deft hands and sharp eyes of the Turkish women creating these never cease to amaze me. Traditionally, Turkish women were brought up to work in the home, learning craft-making skills such as embroidery, knitting and fabric weaving from a young age. In those days, girls possessing highly-developed skills in the arts of craft making were deemed accomplished and hard-working, and were much sought after as wives. When marrying

into a new family, a young girl's "sandık" chest, filled with hand-made oya, became an essential part of her wedding trousseau. Oya was known among the Anatolian women not just for embellishing their own scarves but also to liven up the wardrobes of their husbands', and they often gave oya as gifts to their mothers-in-law, relatives and neighbors. In the days when it was still taboo for women to voice their thoughts and feelings openly in the presence of elder family members, women often wore oya to express their emotions and state of mind. One of the most illustrative examples of this is the "red hot pepper," which brides wore to display feelings of resentment. Oya motifs have been handed down from generation to generation, which is why the names and styles of the motifs vary from region to region. Even today, traditional craft making techniques are being taught to younger generations in places like community centers and female vocational schools, which offer courses in embroidery.

First, make oya to the desired length, and stitch it to the edges of the fabric. You can use the remaining length to lavishly decorate one corner of the fabric (sixth from the top). Small round beads paired with fine yarn lend the oya a delicate and sophisticated feel.

These pieces were drawn from the collection of Mr. and Mrs. Ishimoto. No instructions are provided for the items featured here.

Village hopping in search of Turkish hand-made crafts

Black Sea
Istanbul
Nallıhan
Beypazari
Ankara
Izmir
Cappadocia
Pamukkale
Konya Tarsus
the Mediterranean

❋ The thousand mile journey in pursuit of Turkish oya

Mr. Kanji Ishimoto and Mrs. Chieko Ishimoto fell in love with Turkey and its people while still quite young. Ever since, they have dedicated themselves to promoting Japan-Turkey international relations at the grass-roots level through extensive cultural exchanges. They are also avid collectors of oya. For more than 20 years, they have continually added to their enormous collection of oya, purely out of a passion for the delicate handiwork of the beautiful oya scarves. In 2002, they resolved to hold an exhibition called "Traditional Turkish Embroideries and Oya" at Bunka Women's University in conjunction with the "2003: Turkey Year in Japan." To better showcase their collection professionally and in a methodical way, they adopted a more systematic approach in its assembly, undertaking much of the required research themselves, as well as seeking advice from renowned experts.

They discovered that Iğne oyas are still being made in Southeast Anatolian provinces such as Iğdır, Kahramanmaraş and Bursa, and Boncuk oyas in the small villages of such provinces as Konya and Balıkesir. Scouring the countryside in search of oya, they visited a range of towns and local villages, from ancient East Anatolian towns like Konya and Tarsus to Nallıhan, a small hamlet about 40-50 kilometers (31 miles) from the capital of Ankara. They were blessed with some serendipitous encounters during the long journey. For instance, one day they hailed a taxi and inquired of the driver whether he knew anyone who could make oya. Much to their surprise, he happily replied that his wife was actually an oya maker. On another occasion, they spotted an oya hanging from the ceiling of an old shop, covered in dust. Upon closer examination, it turned out to be a 70-80 year old silk oya of considerable value.

In the autumn of 2003, they invited Prof. Dr. Taciser Onuk (Chairman of the Atatürk Culture Center, Professor at Gazi University), Ms. Türkan Sevgi (former embroidery teacher at a female vocational school) and Ms. Sevgi Şenol (Boncuk Oya researcher) to Japan to hold an oya workshop and exhibition. With these renowned researchers and ambassadors of oya in attendance, the workshop and exhibition proved to be a huge success.

[from top left] A lace maker on the street of Cappadocia/Cappadocia is world-renowned for its unusual rock formations/"Netsuke" (a traditional Japanese accessory) workshop in Beypazari/A warm welcome from girls dressed in traditional attire/A carpet vendor/A temple in Konya

❁ People woven together with the thread of the oya

I first learned about oya whilst leafing through a Western magazine I happened to pick up ten years ago. However, it was not until Mr. and Mrs. Ishimoto's exhibition that I saw oya with my own eyes. Oya, with its beauty and diversity, utterly shook me to the core.

In 2006, Mr. & Mrs. Ishimoto invited me to a cultural exchange tour, which I eagerly joined with my friend K, who is a keen crafter. The main objective being to introduce Japanese culture at a local festival in the town of Beypazarı, which originated as an ancient stop on the Silk Road. While helping with the workshops on Japanese drums, flower arrangement, tea ceremony, calligraphy, "origami" paper crafts and "kimekomi" wooden dolls, we managed to squeeze out some time for a visit to the town hall to partake in a Turkish craft lesson. Ms. Suna and Ms. Satie were our capable teachers. We couldn't speak a word of their language, but it didn't matter in the slightest. Ms. Suna imparted to my friend K the secret of the "Tel Kırma" stitch, a type of embroidery

with silver wire, which we had never seen in Japan. I, on the other hand, worked on Iğne oya with the help of Ms. Satie. Partly due to time restrictions, the finished product wasn't quite as good as I had hoped it would be, but my teachers kindly consoled me and praised my work, saying it was "Çok güzel (very beautiful)". During my stay, I was also fortunate enough to be able to thoroughly peruse the vast collection of exquisite handmade crafts exhibited at the town hall for the duration of the festival, as well as to purchase some oyas from the local craftspeople. Ms. Suna later escorted me to her husband's craft shop, where I encountered and purchased rare yarn and magazines.

Following this, we stopped by the historic town of Konya on a sightseeing tour. In the past, Konya was the center of the Islamic World, and today remains a very religious city. The magnificent mosque swarmed with people, and all women present were wrapped in delightful scarves trimmed with oya. So tempting was

the oya for me that I barely overcame the desire to follow these women and harangue them with questions... What materials do you use? What techniques? How do you crochet? How I wished I could speak Turkish! Even after my return to Japan, my passion for Turkey, or to be more exact, for oya, grew by the day. I took apart a piece of Boncuk oya I had bought at a souvenir shop in Cappadocia to decipher how it was made. With this insight in mind, I made the "grape" choker on p. 36 using beads of my favorite colors. To uncover the hidden secrets of oya, I scrutinized literally every inch of the motifs my friends had given me as well as the ones on the scarves I had purchased, and desperately tried to translate Turkish books and textbooks on the subject with the help of a Turkish dictionary, a present from Mrs. Satie. The deeper I delved into oya, the more determined I became to share the charm of Turkish Boncuk oya and the pleasure of making it with as many people as I could.

[from left to right] A blue mosque with beautifully patterned tiles/The Bosporus Straits/A souvenir shop in Istanbul/A scarf shop/A woman wearing a scarf at the Egyptian Bazaar

Local photos contributed by Yuko Ueki, Taku Nishizawa and Kuma Imamura

Materials & Tools

Here you will find the beads, yarn and tools used in the edging techniques with beads introduced in this book. Find the best combination for the material to be edged and your idea of how you would like the piece to end up.

Round beads
(TOHO seed beads, 12/0 to 7/0)

Round shape beads are the most popular in use. Threaded beads are useful when using beads of one color, or many beads of one color for 1 motif. Join them with yarn and they can be easily moved about. A variety of processed beads such as clear beads, matte beads and aurora beads are available and you can enjoy working with a wide range of different textures.

Bugle beads

Spindly bugle beads resemble bamboo. 3mm-long bugle beads are commonly used, and 6mm-long and 9mm-long bugle beads also exist. Use the best length for the design to be made. The result will be different depending on the length of the bead, even when the motif is the same.

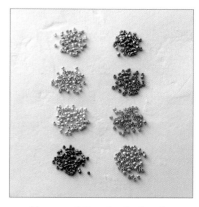

Treasure & Royal color beads
(TOHO cylinder seed beads)

Treasure beads are seed beads produced by TOHO. They are thin cylinder seed beads and often used for embroidery involving beads and bead looming. The royal color beads are also seed beads produced by TOHO. They include round, bugle and 3-cut beads that have unique colors which are rich and mellow.

Special beads

A variety of processed beads in many different colors and shapes are available. Magatama beads and Czech beads will lend a hint of originality to any work. Jujube glass beads are useful in completing certain lengths, similar to bugle beads.

Wood beads

The smallest wood beads of 3mm (1/8") are excellently matched with wool. Washable glossy types and natural matte types are also available. Enjoy mixing and matching colors.

Spangles (Sequins)

Flat and round types of sequins with smooth faces are often utilized in the pieces presented in this book. Dry-cleanable types are also available and can be used for wearable items such as skirts and shirts.

• Contact TOHO Co., Ltd. for inquiries about beads, beading needles and yarn. http://thobeads.net/

Lace yarn

Embroidery thread

Hemp yarn

Wool embroidery thread

Lace yarn
The finest yarn used for the pieces shown in this book is DMC Special Dentelles (meaning "lace" in Turkish, 1 spool is approx. 97m [318' 2-7/8"] long). Since various thicknesses of yarns are available with DMC Cebelia, use the appropriate type for each item. Lace yarn is excellent for seed beads.

Embroidery thread
The Cotton Pearl series produced by DMC possesses a soft, silky texture reminiscent of pearls. A number of colors are available and finding a suitable one isn't difficult. This is a superior choice for beginners, as it is thicker than lace yarn and much easier to crochet.

Wool embroidery thread
100-percent-wool embroidery thread is twisted a bit loosely compared with general embroidery thread. It maintains a fluffy texture, and it is generally recommended to crochet it in a loose manner, unlike with lace yarn. A wide palette of colors is available. Colorful combinations with wood beads are often favored. One skein is approx. 20m (65' 7 3/8") long.

Hemp yarn
An open crochet piece will be made with leather sewing hemp thread. Orizuru-brand hemp yarn for buttons possesses a fine gloss. You can cultivate a natural or wild look, depending upon your chosen beads.

Thread and needles for beading
Nylon thread for beading is fine and stretchy, allowing the crafter to tighten the beads firmly. It is good for use with beading needles. The beading needle shown to the left in the picture is extremely effective for threading beads with a thick thread. Keep one for use with crochet hooks.

Crochet hooks
In this book, a crochet hook No. 10 (0.75mm) is used for lace yarn such as Dentelles, and No. 4 (1.25mm) - No. 8 (0.9mm) is used for wool embroidery thread and slightly thicker hemp yarn. If your crochet work turns out a bit loose, try a thinner hook.

Window-Box

p. 4

Beaded edging for a spring colored scarf

- Size of scarf: 50 x 168cm (19 3/4 x 66") • Width of each motif: 1.1cm (3/8")
- Width of 10 motifs: Approx. 15cm (6") • Make 2 pieces of approx. 168cm (66") beading edging.

Material	Type/Product No.	Amount used		
		1 motif	10 motifs	Total
Yarn	DMC Special Dentelles #80/3687 (pink)	Approx. 27cm (10 3/4")	Approx. 270cm (10.6 1/4")	Approx. 605cm (238 1/8")
Beads	6mm-long bugle bead No.1402 (white)	2	20	448
	Round, 11/0 (2.2mm), No.356 (pink)	5	50	1120
Needle	Crochet hook, No.10 (0.75mm)	–	–	–

* Regarding the yarn, the lengths shown under 'Quantity' are for reference only.

* Allow 20 to 30cm (7 to 12") of yarn for the beginning and end of each row of the crocheting.

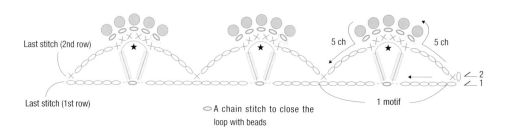

Last stitch (2nd row)

5 ch   5 ch

Last stitch (1st row)

1 motif

A chain stitch to close the loop with beads

Before starting;

Thread the beads on the yarn separately for the 1st and 2nd rows.

1st row (2 per motif)

2 beads   Starting end

2nd row (5 per motif)

5 beads   Starting end

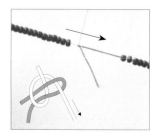

When using single colored beads, tie the bead-thread to the yarn in a sheet bend knot. Transfer beads by sliding.

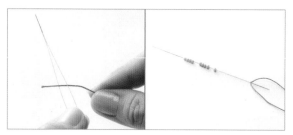

When using many colored loose beads, use a full-eye (Big Eye) needle. As the eye is the full length of the needle shaft, it is useful for any size of thread/yarn.

*To clarify the instructions, different colors are used for the beads and yarn.

*For crocheting symbols and instructions, please refer to p. 63 (chain), p. 65 (double crochet), p. 66 (single crochet) and p. 72 (slip stitch).

1st Row: Crochet 'plant pots' using bugle beads

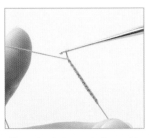

1 Make 6 chain stitches with a beaded yarn.

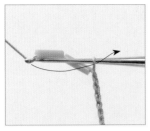

2 Take 2 bugle beads, make a loop and close it with 1 chain stitch.

3 Crochet tightly making sure the 2 beads are close together.

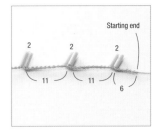

4 Repeat; 11 chain stitches → take/loop 2 beads → 1 chain stitch, to the required length and finish with 6 chain stitches.

2nd Row: Crochet 'flowers' using round beads

1 Join the beaded yarn to the first stitch of the 1st row, make 1 chain stitch and then 1 single crochet.

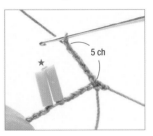

2 Make 5 chain stitches.

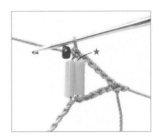

3 Make 1 single crochet between the bugle beads, then take 1 round bead.

4 Make 1 chain stitch to fix the bead, then 1 single crochet at ★.

5 Repeat 4 times to crochet a total of 5 beads; take 1 bead → make 1 chain stitch → make 1 single crochet.

6 Make 5 chain stitches.

7 Make 1 single crochet while wrapping around the 11th chain loop of the 1st row.

8 Repeat steps 2. to 7. to the end. Finish by making 1 single crochet in the last chain.

Completed!

p. 20

design-9
Enchanting Wild Roses

Beaded edging for a sweater

- Width of each motif: 1.8cm (3/4") • 10 motifs: Approx. 65cm (25 5/8")
- Size of edging - Neckline (14 motifs): Approx. 91cm (35 7/8"), Sleeve (6 motifs): Approx. 39cm (15 3/8") x 2

Material	Type/Product No.	Quantity		
		1 motif	10 motifs	Total
Yarn	DMC Special Dentelles #80/743 (yellow)	Approx. 2.7m (8' 10 1/4")	Approx. 27m (88' 7")	Approx. 54m (177' 2")
Beads	Round, 11/0 (2.2mm), No.165 (orange)	93	930	930
	Round, 11/0 (2.2mm), No.946 (lime green)	93	930	930
Needle	Crochet hook, No.10 (0.75mm)	–	–	–

* Regarding yarn, the lengths shown under "Quantity" are for reference only.
* Allow 20 to 30cm (7 to 12") of yarn for the beginning and end of each row of crocheting.

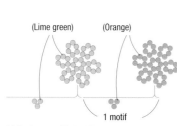

(Lime green)   (Orange)

1 motif

Make two motifs in different alternating colors.

*To simplify the instructions, different colors are used for the beads and yarn.

*For crocheting symbols and instructions, please refer to p. 63 (chain), p. 65 (double crochet), p. 66 (single crochet) and p. 72 (slip stitch).

Tips

Unlike general motifs, this motif should be made from bottom to top.

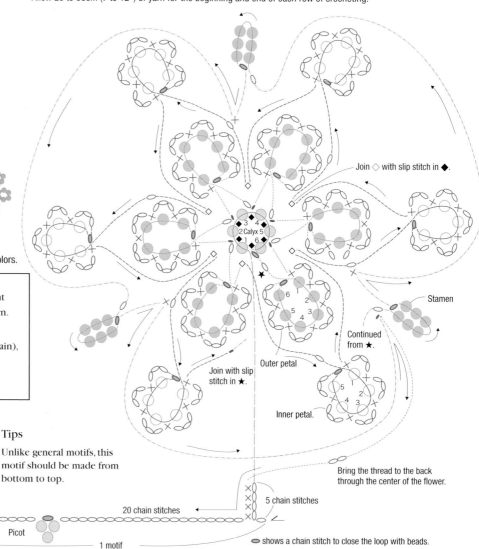

Join ◇ with slip stitch in ◆.

Stamen

Continued from ★.

Outer petal.

Join with slip stitch in ★.

Inner petal.

Bring the thread to the back through the center of the flower.

Stem

20 chain stitches   20 chain stitches

5 chain stitches

Picot

1 motif

◯ shows a chain stitch to close the loop with beads.

Before getting started...

Thread all necessary beads onto a length of yarn.
Double-check the bead order and numbers needed to thread when using multiple colors.
• Bead order and numbers needed to thread for a motif:
  3 for a picot → 18 for 3 stamens → 30 for 6 inner petals → 36 for 6 outer petals → 6 for a calyx (Total: 93 beads)

Picot (3 beads)
Stamens (18 beads)
Inner petals (30 beads)
Outer petals (36 beads)
Calyx (6 beads)
Yarn at the starting end

* For the sweater on page 20, thread 93 lime green beads and 93 orange beads alternately.

For the sweater on page 20

⬤ Crochet Chain Stitch

1 Wrap the yarn over the crochet hook, pulling the yarn in the direction of the arrow.

2 Taking the yarn, draw the hook backward to pull the yarn in the direction of the arrow to close the knot.

3 Draw the hook backward to pull the yarn through the slip knot to make the 1st chain stitch.

Slip knot

4 Repeat step 3 to make the required number of chain stitches. The slip knot is not counted as a chain stitch.

4 chain stitches
Slip knot

1. ⬤ Make a calyx that will be the base (with 6 beads).

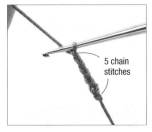

5 chain stitches

1 Make 5 chain stitches.

6 beads

2 Take 6 beads (for a calyx).

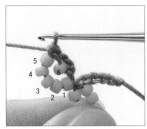

3 Make a loop with the beads and close it with a chain stitch. The outer and inner petals will be joined with a slip stitch in ◆ (see diagram note).

2. ⬤ Make an outer petal (with 6 beads).

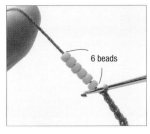

1 Make a chain stitch, take 6 beads, make a loop with the beads and close it with a chain stitch.

2 Make 3 chain stitches, and make a single crochet between the 5th and 6th beads to make a loop.

3 A loop is completed.

4 Repeat to make loops for the other 5 beads, and insert the hook in ◆ (between the 5th and 6th beads for a calyx).

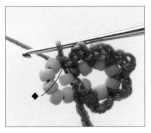

5 Join with a slip stitch to complete a petal.

6 Repeat steps 2-1 to 2-5 and make 5 more petals.

7 When the 6th petal is completed, join it with a slip stitch in between the beads for a calyx.

8 Close the slip stitch a little snugly, and an outer petal is completed.

An example of another application (see the square card on page 53)

- Thread: Olympus Emmy Grande, No. 155 (dark pink)
- Beads: Round bead, No. 559 (platinum) & small round bead, No. 221 (browny gold)
- Thread beads (in the following order: 18 browny gold beads, 72 platinum beads), make a motif, and arrange chain stitches for the length suitable for the card size:.

3. ◯ Make inner petals (with 5 beads each) on outer petals.

1 Make a chain stitch, take 5 beads, make a loop with the beads and close it with 1 chain stitch.

2 As in steps 2-2 to 2-4 for an outer petal, make a petal and join it with a slip stitch in ◆.

3 Make 5 more petals, and join the 6th petal with a slip stitch in between the beads for a calyx.

4 Close the slip stitch a little snugly, and an inner petal is completed.

4. ⬤ Join stamens (with 6 beads each) .

1 Make a chain stitch, form a loop with 6 beads and close it with 1 chain stitch.

2 Join it with a slip stitch in a chain stitch to the base of inner petals (between the 1st and 2nd petals).

3 Make 2 more stamens; join the one with a slip stitch in a chain between the 3rd and 4th petals; place the other in between the 5th and 6th petals.

4 3 stamens are joined with the center of the flower. Make 2 chain stitches and bring them to the back side through the center.

5. ◯ Make a stem and a picot (with 3 beads) .

1 Cover the beginning chain stitches with 4 single crochets.

2 Make 20 chain stitches, add 3 beads, close the loop of beads with a chain stitch, make 20 more chain stitches, and a motif is completed.

Yarn at the starting end

All done!

With this motif, you can create a variety of color combinations, for example using similar colors for the inner and outer petals and different colors for the 3 stamens.

design-2
Orchard

p.6

Beaded edging for a T-shirt

- Width of each motif: 0.9cm (3/8") • 10 motifs: Approx. 7cm (2 3/4")
- Size of edging - Neckline (118 motifs): Approx. 82.6cm (32 1/2"), Sleeve edge (29 motifs): Approx. 20.3cm (8") x 2

Material	Type/Product No.	Amount used		
		1 motif	10 motifs	Total
Yarn	DMC Special Dentelles #80/3778 (orange)	Approx. 10cm (3 7/8")	Approx. 1m (3' 3 7/8")	Approx. 17.6m (57' 8 7/8")
Beads	Round, 8/0 (3.0mm), No.125 (red)	3	30	528
	Round, 8/0 (3.0mm), No.262 (gold)	1	10	176
Needle	Crochet hook, No.10 (0.75mm)	–	–	–

* Regarding yarn, the lengths shown under "Quantity" are for reference only.

* Allow 20 to 30cm (7 to 12") of yarn for the beginning and end of each row of crocheting.

How to thread the beads

1st row

1 motif

(Red) 3 beads (Red) 3 beads (Red) 3 beads

Starting end

2nd row

1 motif

(Gold) 1 bead (Gold) 1 bead (Gold) 1 bead

Starting end

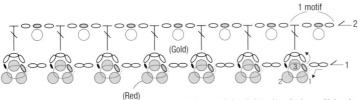

(Gold)

(Red)

1 motif

2

1

⊙ shows a chain stitch to close the loop with beads.

1 Measure the length of the part to be edged, and calculate the required number of motifs and beads based on the table above. Depending on the creator, the crochet work may be shorter than the size shown in the table, so thread enough extra beads onto the yarn to make at least five motifs.

2 Thread beads onto the yarn for the 1st row.
  • 1 motif: Red beads x 3

3 Make 2 chain stitches, take 3 beads and close it with a chain stitch.

4 Make 3 chain stitches, join it to the part between the 2nd and 3rd beads in step 3 with a slip stitch to make a loop.

5 Repeat steps 3 to 4 until the required length is reached.

6 Thread the beads onto the yarn for the 2nd row.
  • 1 motif: Gold bead x 1

7 Make 1 chain stitch, take 1 bead and make 1 chain stitch to fix it in place, and make 1 more chain stitch.

8 Make 1 double crochet on the loop of three chain stitches on the 1st row.

9 Repeat steps 7 to 8 until finished

⊤ Double crochet

1 Make 3 chain stitches, wrap the yarn over the hook, and insert the hook in the fourth chain from the hook.

First 3 chain stitches

2 Wrap the yarn over the hook again and draw the yarn in the direction of the arrow.

3 Wrap the yarn over the hook and draw it through the two loops as indicated by the arrow in the figure.

4 Wrap the yarn over the hook again and draw it through the two loops.

5 One double crochet is completed. Count the first 3 chain stitches as the first double crochet stitch.

design-3

Refreshing Breeze

p. 8

Beaded edging for a blouse

- Width of each motif: 1.4cm (1/2")   • 10 motifs: Approx. 13cm (5 1/8")
- Size of edging - Neckline (36 motifs): Approx. 47cm (18 1/2"), Sleeve edge (16 motifs): Approx. 23cm (9") x 2

Material	Type/Product No.	Amount used		
		1 motif	10 motifs	Total
Yarn	DMC Cebelia #30/3865 (white)	Approx. 40cm (15 3/4")	Approx. 4m (13' 1 1/2")	Approx. 27.5m (90' 2 5/8")
Beads	Round, 11/0 (2.2mm), No.23 (aqua)	4	40	272
	Round, 11/0 (2.2mm), No.262 (gold)	7	70	476
Needle	Crochet hook, No.10 (0.75mm)	–	–	–

* Regarding yarn, the lengths shown under "Quantity" are for reference only.

* Allow 20 to 30cm (7 to 12") of yarn for the beginning and end of each row of crocheting.

Threading the beads

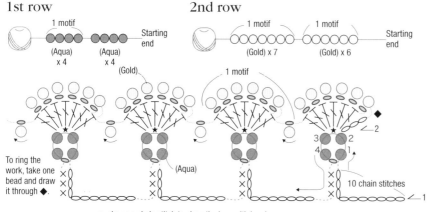

shows a chain stitch to close the loop with beads.

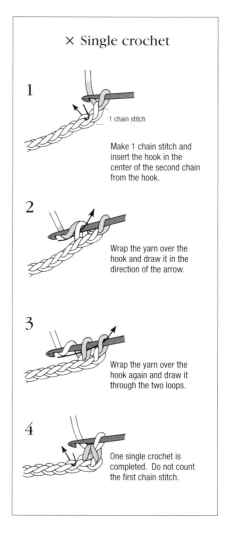

× **Single crochet**

1

1 chain stitch

Make 1 chain stitch and insert the hook in the center of the second chain from the hook.

2

Wrap the yarn over the hook and draw it in the direction of the arrow.

3

Wrap the yarn over the hook again and draw it through the two loops.

4

One single crochet is completed. Do not count the first chain stitch.

1 Measure the length of the part to be edged and calculate the required number of motifs and beads based on the table above. Depending on the individual, the crochet work may be shorter than the size shown in the table, so thread enough extra beads onto the yarn to make at least three or four motifs.

2 Thread the beads onto the yarn for the 1st row.
- 4 beads per motif (aqua)

3 Make 10 chain stitches, take 4 beads and then close it with a chain stitch.

4 Make 3 single crochets using the 3 chain stitches of step 3.

5 Repeat steps 3 to 4 until the required length is reached.

6 Thread the beads onto the yarn for the 2nd row.
- 7 beads (gold) per motif (6 beads for the first motif)

7 Join the beaded yarn to ★ (between the 2nd bead and the 3rd) of the 1st row, then make 3 chain stitches.

8 Take 1 bead and make 1 chain stitch to fix the bead, and 1 double crochet at ★. Repeat 5 times to fix a total of 6 beads.

9 Take 1 bead and make 1 chain stitch to fix the bead, and 1 double crochet at ★ of the next 4 beads. Repeat 6 times to fix a total of 7 beads.

10 Repeat step 9 to the end.

design-4

Dew Drops in the Meadow

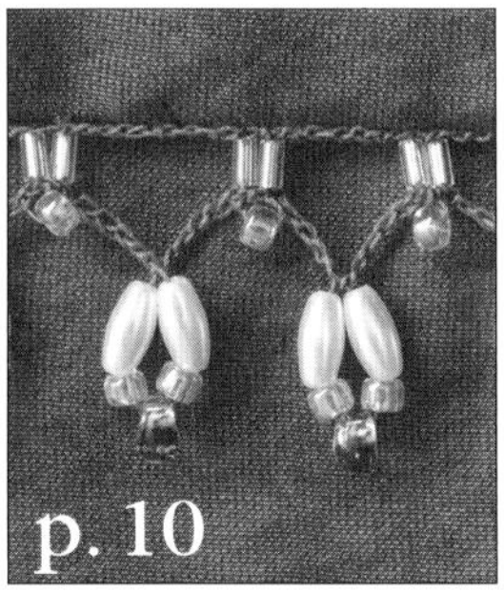

Beaded edging for a skirt

- Width of each motif: 2.3cm (7/8") • 10 motifs: Approx. 13cm (5 1/8")
- Size of edging - (119 motifs): Approx. 1.55m (5' 1")

Material	Type/Product No.	Amount used		
		1 motif	10 motifs	Total
Yarn	DMC Special Dentelles #80/799 (blue)	Approx. 18cm (7-1/8")	Approx. 1.8m (5' 10-7/8")	Approx. 21.5m (70' 61/2")
Beads	3mm-long bugle beads, No.21 (silver)	2	20	238
	Round, 8/0 (3.0mm), No.170 (aqua)	3	30	357
	Jujube glass bead, pearl, No.200 (3 x 6mm), No.200 (pearl white)	2	20	238
	Magatama bead, No.M23 (aqua)	1	10	119
Needle	Crochet hook, No.10 (0.75mm)	–	–	–

* Regarding yarn, the lengths shown under "Quantity" are for reference only.

* Allow 20 to 30cm (7 to 12") of yarn for the beginning and end of each row of crocheting.

Threading the beads

1st row

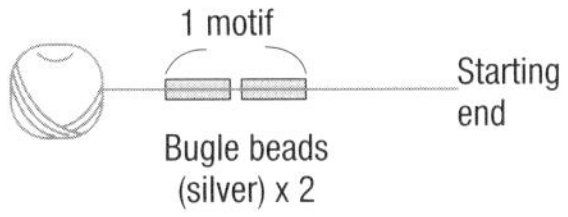

2nd row

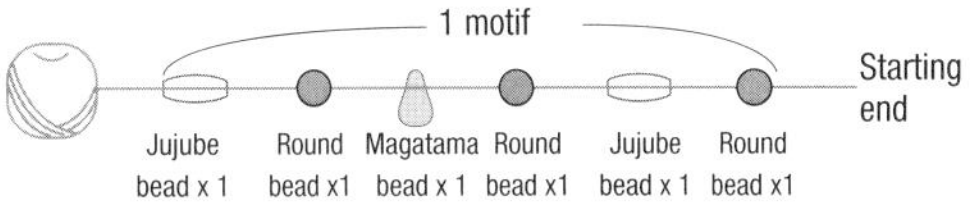

• To ring the work

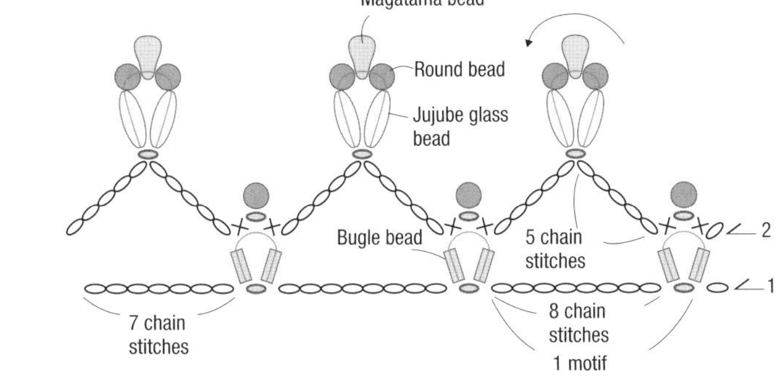

• To make flat

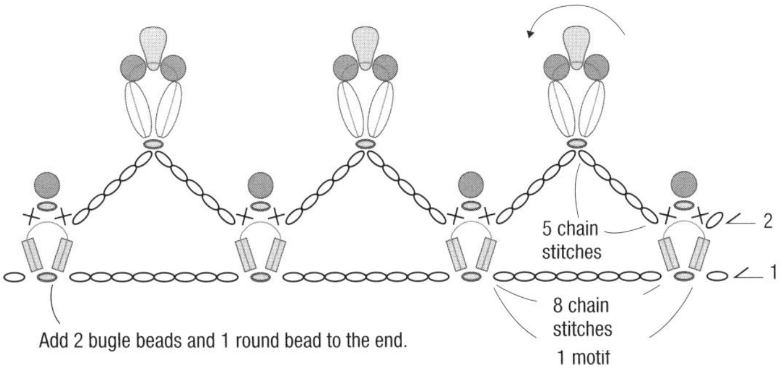

⬭ shows a chain stitch to close the loop with beads.

1 Measure the length of the part to be edged and calculate the required number of motifs and beads based on the table above. Depending on the individual, the crochet work may be shorter than the size shown in the table, so thread enough extra beads onto the yarn to make at least three or four motifs.

2 Thread the beads onto the yarn.
• 2 bugle beads (silver) per motif

3 For the 1st row, repeat the following steps until the required length is reached: (with 1 chain stitch at the starting end) take 2 bugle beads and close it with 1 chain stitch; make 8 chain stitches. Repeat until required length is reached, ending with 7 chain stitches to ring the work. To make flat, make 1 chain stitch at the starting end and the finishing end.

4 Thread the beads onto the yarn for the 2nd row.
• 1 motif: 1 jujube glass bead → 1 round bead → 1 Magatama bead → 1 round bead → 1 jujube glass bead → 1 round bead

5 Join the beaded yarn to the part between the bugle beads of the 1st row and make 1 chain stitch and 1 single crochet. Take 1 round bead and make 1 chain stitch to fix the bead, then make 1 single crochet between the bugle beads.

6 Make 5 chain stitches, take 5 beads and close it with a chain stitch, then make 5 chain stitches.

7 Repeat the following steps to the end: make 1 single crochet between the next bugle beads→ take 1 bead and close it with a chain stitch → 1 single crochet → 5 chain stitches → take 5 beads and close it with a chain stitch → 5 chain stitches.

Fluttering Butterflies

* Regarding yarn, the lengths shown under 'Quantity' are for reference only.
* Allow 20 to 30cm (7 to 12") of yarn for the beginning and end of each row of crocheting.

Summery hat decoration

- Width of each motif: 2.7cm (1 1/8")
- 10 motifs: Approx. 49.5cm (19 1/2")
- Size of edging - (24 motifs): Approx. 1.2m (3' 11 1/4")

Material	Type/Product No.	Amount used		
		1 motif	10 motifs	Total
Yarn	DMC Cebelia #30/3865 (white)	Approx. 1.74m (5' 8 1/2")	Approx. 17.4m (57' 1")	Approx. 42m (137' 9 1/2")
Beads	Round, 11/0 (2.2mm), No.174 (orange)	40	400	240
	Round, 11/0 (2.2mm), No.192 (yellow)	40	400	240
	Round, 11/0 (2.2mm), No.165 (red)	40	400	240
	Round, 11/0 (2.2mm), No.105 (lime green)	40	400	240
	Round, 11/0 (2.2mm), No.85 (purple)	8	80	192
	Round, 11/0 (2.2mm), No.947 (green)	4	40	92
Needle	Crochet hook, No.8 (0.90mm)	–	–	–

Use 1 of the 4 colors for 1 motif. (spanning the orange/yellow/red/lime green rows)

Threading the beads

1 motif

(Green) x 4   (Purple) x 4   (Orange/red/lime green/yellow) 40 beads Use 1 color per motif. Repeat 4 motifs.   (Purple) x 4   Starting end

1 Calculate the required number of motifs and beads based on the table above. Thread the beads onto the yarn based on the figure above.

2 Make 6 chain stitches, then take 4 (purple) beads and close it with a chain stitch.

3 Make 1 chain stitch, take 10 beads (the wing of the butterfly) and close it with a chain stitch, then join it with a slip stitch in between the beads of step 2.

4 Repeat step 3 three times to make four wings, then join the 4th wing with slip stitch to ◆ (a chain stitch closing 4 beads).

5 Make 6 chain stitches, then make 1 single crochet in the center of the wing (between the 5th and the 6th beads).

6 Make 3 picots of 3 chain stitches with 1 single crochet.

7 Make 2 chain stitches, then make 1 single crochet in the center of the next wing. Make 3 picots as in step 6 then make 6 chain stitches.

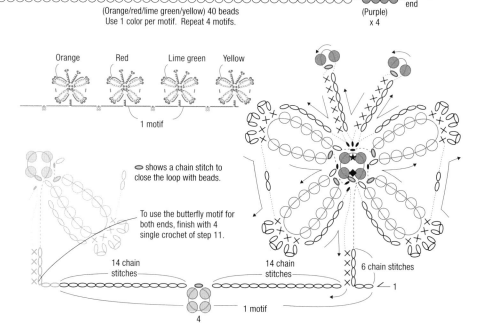

Orange   Red   Lime green   Yellow

1 motif

◯ shows a chain stitch to close the loop with beads.

To use the butterfly motif for both ends, finish with 4 single crochet of step 11.

14 chain stitches   14 chain stitches   6 chain stitches

1 motif

8 Join it with a slip stitch to ★ and make 6 chain stitches. Take 2 (purple) beads and close it with a chain stitch, then make 6 single crochets using the 6 chain stitches.

9 Repeat step 8 and join it with a slip stitch to ★ to make two antennas.

10 Repeat steps 5 to 7 to complete the wings and join it with a slip stitch to ◆.

11 Make 4 single crochets using the 4 chain stitches in step 2. Make 14 chain stitches, take 4 (green) beads and close it with a chain stitch, then make 14 chain stitches.

Church Bells

p. 14

Lariat with linen yarn

- Width of each motif: 2.7cm (1 1/8")
- 10 motifs: Approx. 55cm (21 5/8")
- Size of edging - (48 motifs): Approx. 2.6m (8' 6 3/8")

Material	Type/Product No.		Amount used		
			1 motif	10 motifs	Total
Yarn	Hemp yarn (beige)		Approx. 125cm (4' 1 1/4")	Approx. 12.5m (41' 1/8")	Approx. 60m (196' 10 1/4")
Beads	Round, 8/0 (3.0mm), No.50 (orange)	Use 1 of the 4 colors for 1 motif.	30	300	360
	Round, 8/0 (3.0mm), No.42 (yellow)		30	300	357
	Round, 8/0 (3.0mm), No.45 (red)		30	300	360
	Round, 8/0 (3.0mm), No.47 (green)		30	300	360
Needle	Crochet hook, No.8 (0.90mm)		–	–	–

Threading the beads

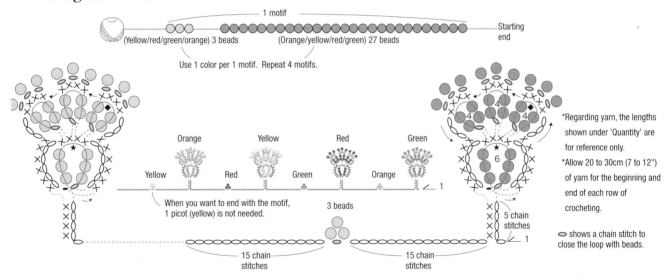

1 motif

(Yellow/red/green/orange) 3 beads   (Orange/yellow/red/green) 27 beads   Starting end

Use 1 color per 1 motif. Repeat 4 motifs.

Orange   Yellow   Red   Green

Yellow   Red   Green   Orange

When you want to end with the motif, 1 picot (yellow) is not needed.

3 beads

15 chain stitches   15 chain stitches

5 chain stitches

*Regarding yarn, the lengths shown under 'Quantity' are for reference only.

*Allow 20 to 30cm (7 to 12") of yarn for the beginning and end of each row of crocheting.

⬯ shows a chain stitch to close the loop with beads.

1 Calculate the required number of motifs and beads based on the table above. Thread the beads onto the yarn based on the figure above.

2 Make 5 chain stitches, then take 6 beads and close it with a chain stitch.

3 Make 6 chain stitches, then make 1 single crochet at ★ (between the 3rd and 4th beads).

4 Take 4 beads and close it with a chain stitch and make 1 single crochet at ★. Repeat twice to make 3 squares.

5 Make 6 chain stitches, then join it with a slip stitch to the point closing the 6 beads.

6 Make 6 single crochets using the chain stitches in step 3, then make 3 chain stitches.

7 Make 1 single crochet at ◆ (between the 2nd and 3rd beads).

8 Take 1 bead and make 1 chain stitch, then make 1 single crochet at ◆. Repeat twice to fix a total of 3 beads.

9 Repeat steps 7 to 8 to fix 3 beads per square.

10 Make 3 chain stitches, then make 6 single crochets using the chain stitches of step 5. Make 4 single crochets using the chain stitches of step 2.

11 Make 15 chain stitches, take 3 beads and close it with a chain stitch, then make 15 chain stitches.

12 Repeat steps 2 to 11 until the required length is reached. End with step 10 omitting 1 picot.

Dainty Berries

p. 16

Beaded edging for a camisole

- Width of each motif: 1.3cm (1/2") • 10 motifs: Approx. 40cm (15 3/4")
- Size of edging - (7 motifs): Approx. 25cm (9 7/8") x 2

Material	Type/Product No.	Amount used		
		1 motif	10 motifs	Total
Yarn	DMC Special Dentelles #80/3052 (moss green)	Approx. 57cm (22 1/2")	Approx. 5.7m (18' 8 3/8")	Approx. 8m (26' 3")
Beads	Round, 11/0 (2.2mm), No.332 (purple-red)	24	240	336
	Round, 11/0 (2.2mm), No.246 (green)	26	260	352
Needle	Crochet hook, No.10 (0.75mm)	–	–	–

Threading the beads

1 motif

(Green) x 6   (Green) x 16   (Purple-red) x 24   (Green) x 4   Starting end

Not necessary when finishing with motif.

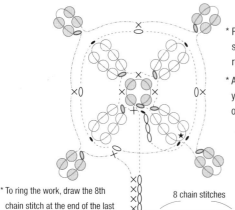

* Regarding yarn, the lengths shown under "Quantity" are for reference only.

* Allow 20 to 30cm (7 to 12") of yarn for the beginning and end of each row of crocheting.

* When you want to end with the berry motif, the last 2 picots are not needed.

* To ring the work, draw the 8th chain stitch at the end of the last motif through the starting stitch.

8 chain stitches   8 chain stitches   8 chain stitches   6 chain stitches

⬤ shows a chain stitch to close the loop with beads.

1 motif

1 Measure the length of the part to be edged; calculate the required number of motifs and beads based on the table above, then thread the beads onto the yarn.
- 1 motif: (Green) x 6 → (green) 16 beads → (purple-red) 24 beads → (green) 4 beads
Depending on the individual, the crochet work may be shorter than the size shown in the table, so thread extra beads onto the yarns to make at least one motif. When you want to end with the berry motif, the first 6 (green) beads for 2 picots are not needed.

2 Make 6 chain stitches, then take 4 (green) beads and close it with a chain stitch.

3 Take 6 (purple-red) beads and close it with a chain stitch, then make 1 single crochet between the beads in step 2. Repeat three times to make a total of 4 sets of 6 beads, then join it with slip stitch to the chain stitch closing the 4 green beads.

4 Make 3 chain stitches. -These chain stitches will be hidden in the berry motif.

5 Join it with a slip stitch at ★ (between the 3rd and the 4th beads) of the 6 beads, then make 1 chain stitch. Repeat three times. Join it with a slip stitch at ★ again to collect up the purple-red beads. Keep the 6 chain stitches in step 2 in the center of the berry.

6 Take 4 (green) beads and close it with a chain stitch, then make a single crochet on 1 chain stitch in step 5. Repeat three times to make a total of 4 calyxes.

7 Make 4 single crochets using the chain stitches in step 2, then make 8 chain stitches.

8 Take 3 (green) beads and close it with a chain stitch, then make 8 chain stitches. Repeat to make a total of 2 picots with beads.

9 Repeat steps 2. to 8. to the required length. To use the berry motif for both ends, finish with the 4 single crochets as in step 7.

Soap Bubbles

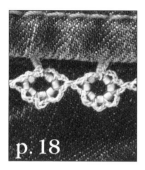

p. 18

Edging jean pocket flaps

- Width of each motif: 1.5cm (5/8")   • 10 motifs: Approx. 10cm (3 7/8")
- Size of edging - (18 motifs): Approx. 18cm (7 1/8") x 2

Material	Type/Product No.	Amount used		
		1 motif	10 motifs	Total
Yarn	DMC Special Dentelles #80/738 (beige)	Approx. 33.5cm (13 1/4")	Approx. 3.35m (10' 11 7/8")	Approx. 12.1m (39' 8 3/8")
Beads	Round, 11/0 (2.2mm), No.931 (aqua)	7	70	252
Needle	Crochet hook, No.10 (0.75mm)	–	–	–

* Regarding yarn, the lengths shown under "Quantity" are for reference only.
* Allow 20 to 30cm (7 to 12") of yarn for the beginning and end of each row of crocheting.

Threading the beads

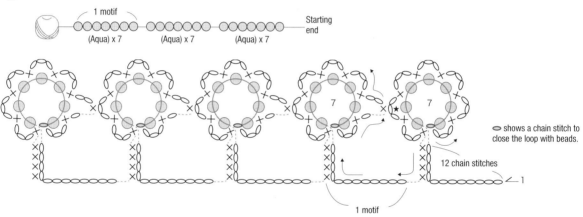

1 motif

(Aqua) x 7   (Aqua) x 7   (Aqua) x 7   Starting end

7   7

★   7

⬭ shows a chain stitch to close the loop with beads.

12 chain stitches

1 motif

1 Measure the length of the part to be edged; and calculate the required number of motifs and beads based on the table above, then thread the beads onto the yarn.
• 7 beads (aqua) per motif
Depending on the individual, the crochet work may be shorter than the size shown in the table, so thread extra beads onto the yarn to make at least three or four motifs.

2 Make 12 chain stitches, then take 7 beads and close it with a chain stitch.

3 Make 3 chain stitches, then make a single crochet between the beads. Repeat 6 times to make a total of 7 loops.

4 Make 4 single crochets using the chain stitches in step 2.

5 Repeat steps 2 to 4 and make a single crochet at ★ of the previous motif when you make the 2nd loop to join the 2 motifs.

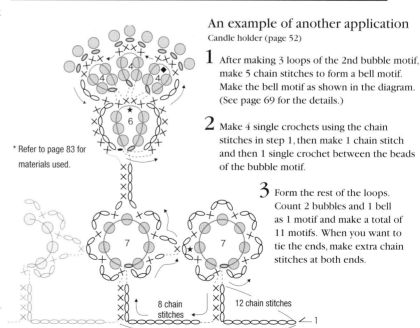

* Refer to page 83 for materials used.

4   4
4
★
6

7   ★   7

8 chain stitches   12 chain stitches

1 motif

An example of another application
Candle holder (page 52)

1 After making 3 loops of the 2nd bubble motif, make 5 chain stitches to form a bell motif. Make the bell motif as shown in the diagram. (See page 69 for the details.)

2 Make 4 single crochets using the chain stitches in step 1, then make 1 chain stitch and then 1 single crochet between the beads of the bubble motif.

3 Form the rest of the loops. Count 2 bubbles and 1 bell as 1 motif and make a total of 11 motifs. When you want to tie the ends, make extra chain stitches at both ends.

A Floral Hedge

Edging jean pocket flaps

p. 22

- Width of each motif: 0.9cm (3/8")   • 10 motifs: Approx. 10cm (3 7/8")
- Size of edging - Cardigan (114 motifs): Approx. 114cm (7 1/8"); Inner knit (72 motifs): Approx. 72cm (28 3/8")

Material	Type/Product No.	Amount used		
		1 motif	10 motifs	Total
Yarn	DMC Special Dentelles #80/3778 (orange)	Approx. 17.5cm (6 7/8")	Approx. 1.75m (5' 8 7/8")	Approx. 33m (108' 3 1/4")
Beads	Round, 11/0 (2.2mm), No.165 (red)	8	80	1488
Needle	Crochet hook, No.10 (0.75mm)	–	–	–

* Regarding yarn, the lengths shown under "Quantity" are for reference only.

* Allow 20 to 30cm (7 to 12") of yarn for the beginning and end of each row of crocheting.

Threading the beads

1 motif

(Red) x 4   (Red) x 4   (Red) x 4   (Red) x 4   Starting end

◯ shows a chain stitch to close the loop with beads.

1 motif
5 chain stitches

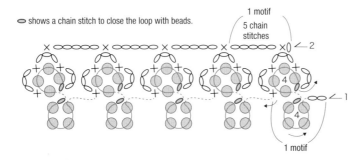

1 motif

1 Measure the length of the part to be edged; calculate the required number of motifs and beads based on the table above, then thread the beads onto the yarn for the 1st row.
• 8 red beads per motif
Depending on the individual, the crochet work may be shorter than the size shown in the table, so thread extra beads onto the yarn to make at least three or four motifs.

2 Make 2 chain stitches for the 1st row.

3 Take 4 beads and close it with a chain stitch, then take 4 beads and close it in the same way.

4 Make 3 chain stitches, then make 1 single crochet between the last and the previous beads. Repeat twice to make 3 loops of 3 chain stitches.

5 Repeat steps 3 to 4 until the required length is reached.

6 For the 2nd row, join the yarn to the 2nd loop of the 1st row, then make 1 chain stitch and 1 single crochet.

7 Make 5 chain stitches and make 1 single crochet at the 2nd loop of the next motif. Repeat to the end. To ring the work, draw the finishing end through the starting stitch.

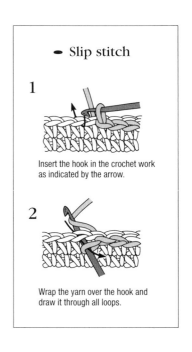

● Slip stitch

1

Insert the hook in the crochet work as indicated by the arrow.

2

Wrap the yarn over the hook and draw it through all loops.

A Garden of Pansies

Beaded edging for a wool camisole

Neckline • Width of each motif: 1.1cm (3/8") • 10 motifs: Approx. 12.5cm (4 7/8")
• Size of edging - (22 motifs): Approx. 27.5cm (10 7/8")

Hem • Width of each motif: 0.8cm (3/8") • 10 motifs: Approx. 10cm (3 7/8")
• Size of edging - (106 motifs): Approx. 106cm (41 3/4")

p.24

	Material	Type/Product No.	Amount used		
			1 motif	10 motifs	Total
Neckline	Yarn	DMC Cebelia #30/989 (moss green)	Approx. 30.5cm (12")	Approx. 3.05m (10' 1/8")	Approx. 6.8m (22' 3 3/4")
	Beads	Round, 8/0 (3.0mm), No.974 (yellow)	4	40	88
		Round, 8/0 (3.0mm), No.264 (purple)	5	50	110
Hem	Yarn	DMC Special Dentelles #80/3052 (moss green)	Approx. 28.5cm (11 1/4")	Approx. 2.85m (9' 4 1/4")	Approx. 30.5m (100' 3/4")
	Beads	Round, 11/0 (2.2mm), No.974 (yellow)	4	40	424
		Round, 11/0 (2.2mm), No.265 (purple)	5	50	530
	Needle	Crochet hook, No.10 (0.75mm)	–	–	–

* Regarding yarn, the lengths shown under "Quantity" are for reference only.

* Allow 20 to 30cm (7 to 12") of yarn for the beginning and end of each row of crocheting.

Threading the beads

1st row

1 motif — (Yellow) x 4 (Yellow) x 4 — Starting end

2nd row

1 motif — (Purple) x 5 (Purple) x 5 — Starting end

* The same for both the neckline and the hem.

⌒ shows a chain stitch to close the loop with beads.

• To make flat

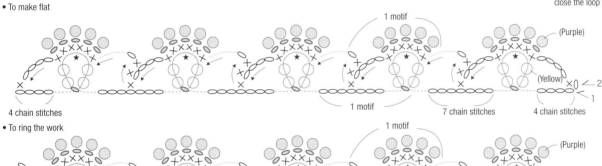

4 chain stitches

1 motif

1 motif

7 chain stitches

4 chain stitches

(Purple)

(Yellow)

• To ring the work

4 chain stitches

1 motif

1 motif

7 chain stitches

3 chain stitches

(Purple)

(Yellow)

1 Measure the length of the part to be edged, and calculate the required number of motifs and beads based on the table above. Depending on the individual, the crochet work may be shorter than the size shown in the table, so thread enough extra beads onto the yarn to make at least three or four motifs.

2 Thread beads onto the yarn for the 1st row.
• 4 yellow beads per motif

3 Make 4 chain stitches.
* Make 3 chain stitches when ringing the work.

4 Take 4 beads and close it with a chain stitch, then make 7 chain stitches. Repeat until the required length is reached.

5 Thread beads onto the yarn for the 2nd row.
• 5 purple beads per motif

6 Join the beaded yarn to the starting end of the 1st row, then make 1 chain stitch and 1 single crochet, and then 4 chain stitches.
* Start from step 7 when ringing the work.

7 Make 1 single crochet at ★. Repeat to fix a total of 5 beads; take 1 bead → make 1 chain stitch → make 1 single crochet.

8 Make 4 chain stitches, then make 1 single crochet in the 4th chain stitch of the 1st row. Make 2 single crochets using 2 of the 4 chain stitches to go back and make 1 chain stitch.

9 Repeat steps 7 to 8 to the end. Make 1 single crochet at the end of the 1st row to finish.

Lace Flowers

p. 26

Beaded edging for a stole

- Width of each motif: 1.6cm (5/8") • 10 motifs: Approx. 23.5cm (9 1/4")
- Size of edging - (76 motifs): Approx. 178.5cm (5' 10 1/4") x 2

Material	Type/Product No.	Amount used		
		1 motif	10 motifs	Total
Yarn	DMC Cebelia #10/ECRU (natural undyed color)	Approx. 80cm (31 1/2")	Approx. 8m (26' 3")	Approx. 122m (400' 3 1/8")
Beads	Round, 8/0 (3.0mm), No.125 (red)	4	40	608
	Round, 8/0 (3.0mm), No.262 (gold)	14	140	2128
Needle	Crochet hook, No.8 (0.90mm)	–	–	–

* Regarding yarn, the lengths shown under "Quantity" are for reference only.

* Allow 20 to 30cm (7 to 12") of yarn for the beginning and end of each row of crocheting.

Threading the beads

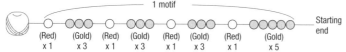

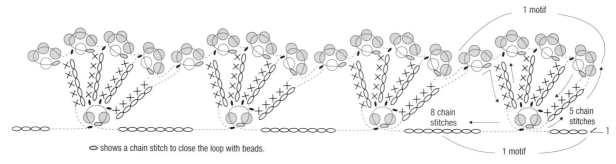

shows a chain stitch to close the loop with beads.

1 Measure the length of the part to be edged and calculate the required number of motifs and beads based on the table above, then thread the beads onto the yarn.
Depending on the individual, the crochet work may be shorter than the size shown in the table, so thread enough extra beads onto the yarn to make at least two motifs.

2 Make 4 chain stitches, then take 2 (gold) beads and close it with a chain stitch.

3 Make 5 chain stitches, then take 4 beads (3 gold beads, 1 red bead) and close it with a chain stitch.

4 Make 5 single crochets using the 5 chain stitches of step 3 to return, and join it with a slip stitch in between the beads of step 2.

5 Make 5 chain stitches, then turn over the crochet work, and join it with a slip stitch in between the red bead and gold bead.

6 Take 4 beads (3 gold beads, 1 red bead) and close it with a chain stitch. Turn over the crochet work again and make 5 single crochets using the 5 chain stitches to return, then join it with a slip stitch in between the beads of step 2.

7 Repeat steps 5. to 6. twice. Make the last slip stitch at the base closing the 2 beads.

8 Make 8 chain stitches, then take and close 2 (gold) beads as in step 2.

9 Make 5 chain stitches and join it with a slip stitch in between the red bead and gold bead of the previous motif (to join 2 motifs), then crochet as in step 6.

10 Repeat step 9 three times to make a total of 4 florets. (Make the last slip stitch at the base closing the 2 beads.)

11 Repeat steps 8. to 10. until the required length is reached. End with 4 chain stitches to make flat. To ring the work, make 4 chain stitches after step 10, then join it with a slip stitch to the starting end.

design-13

Sun-dazzled Footpath

p. 28

Beaded edging for a coat

- Width of each motif: 1.1cm (3/8") • 10 motifs: Approx. 4.5cm (1 3/4")
- Size of edging - (190 motifs): Approx. 85.5cm (33 5/8")

Material	Type/Product No.	Amount used		
		1 motif	10 motifs	Total
Yarn	DMC Cotton Perle #8/902 (purple-red)	Approx. 9.5cm (3 3/4")	Approx. 95cm (37 3/8")	Approx. 18.1m (59' 4 5/8")
Beads	Round, 8/0 (3.0mm), No.333 (green)	3	30	570
	Round, 11/0 (2.2mm), No.105 (lime green)	3	30	570
Needle	Crochet hook, No.8 (0.90mm)	–	–	–

* Regarding yarn, the lengths shown under "Quantity" are for reference only.

* Allow 20 to 30cm (7 to 12") of yarn for the beginning and end of each row of crocheting.

Threading the beads

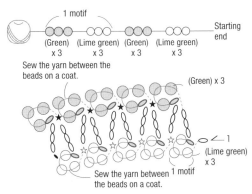

⊖ shows a chain stitch to close the loop with beads.

1 Measure the length of the part to be edged; calculate the required number of motifs and beads based on the table above, then thread the beads onto the yarn.
• 1 motif: Green bead x 3 -> Lime green bead x 3
Depending on the individual, the crochet work may be shorter than the size shown in the table, so thread enough extra beads onto the yarn to make at least six motifs.

2 Make 1 chain stitch, then take 3 (lime green) beads and close it with a chain stitch, and form 3 chain stitches.

3 Take 3 (green) beads and close it with a chain stitch, then make 3 chain stitches. Turn over the crochet work and join it with a slip stitch at ☆ (between the 2nd and the 3rd beads of step 2).

4 Take 3 (lime green) beads and close it with a chain stitch, then turn over the crochet work. Make 3 chain stitches and join it with a slip stitch at ★ (between the 2nd and the 3rd beads of step 3).

5 Repeat steps 3 to 4 until the required length is reached.
* Combining 3 small round beads with 3 round beads, you can create a crochet work with a gentle curve.

---

p. 51	design-13	Summer lariat

Material	Type/Product No.	Amount used	
		1 motif	160 motifs
Yarn	Silk lace yarn No.1 (white)	Approx. 8.2cm (3 1/4")	Approx. 13.2m (43' 3 5/8")
	Braided bead thread (white)		
Beads	Round bead, No.558 (platinum)	3	480
	Round bead, No.264 (turquoise)	3	480
Needle	Crochet hook, No.8/Beading needle	–	–

* Regarding yarn, the lengths shown under "Quantity" are for reference only.

* Allow 20 to 30cm (7 to 12") of yarn for the beginning and end of each row of crocheting.

• Fringe: Spiral bead, 6mm, No. 21 (silver) x 96, treasure bead, No.A-558 (platinum) x 80, round, 8/0 (3.0mm), No. 264 (turquoise) x 48

Threading the beads

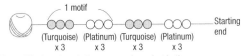

Thread the beads onto the yarn and crochet in the same way as in the beaded edging for a coat. After taking care of the yarn end, join the fringes with braided bead thread to the chain stitches at the end of the crochet work. (Join the fringes to the opposite end in the same way).

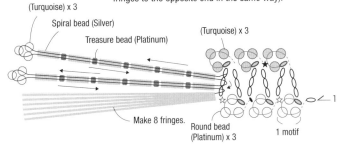

Sparkling Fringe

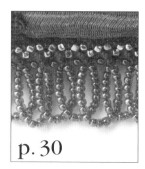

p. 30

Beaded edging for a petite bag

- Width of each motif: 2.2cm (7/8")   • 10 motifs: Approx. 5cm (2")
- Size of edging - (40 motifs): Approx. 20cm (7 7/8")

Material	Type/Product No.	Amount used		
		1 motif	10 motifs	Total
Yarn	DMC Cebelia #30/816 (purple-red)	Approx. 11cm (4 3/8")	Approx. 1.1m (3' 7 1/4")	Approx. 4.4m (14' 5 1/4")
Beads	3-cut bead, No.CR715 (royal color; gold)	3	30	120
	Round, 11/0 (2.2mm), No.356 (purple-red)	20	200	800
Needle	Crochet hook, No.10 (0.75mm)	–	–	–

* Regarding yarn, the lengths shown under "Quantity" are for reference only.

* Allow 20 to 30cm (7 to 12") of yarn for the beginning and end of each row of crocheting.

Threading the beads

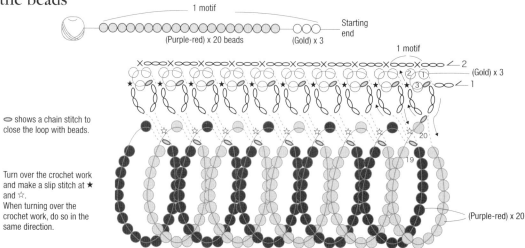

1 motif

(Purple-red) x 20 beads   (Gold) x 3   Starting end

1 motif

(Gold) x 3

⬭ shows a chain stitch to close the loop with beads.

Turn over the crochet work and make a slip stitch at ★ and ☆.
When turning over the crochet work, do so in the same direction.

(Purple-red) x 20

1 Measure the length of the part to be edged; and calculate the required number of motifs and beads based on the table above, then thread the beads onto the yarn for the 1st row.
• 1 motif: Purple-red bead x 20 -> Gold bead x 3
Depending on the individual, the crochet work may be shorter than the size shown in the table, so thread enough extra beads onto the yarn to make at least five to six motifs.

2 Make 2 chain stitches for the 1st row.

3 Take 3 (gold) beads and close it with a chain stitch, then make 3 chain stitches.

4 Take 20 (purple-red) beads and close it with a chain stitch, then make 3 chain stitches.

5 Turn over the crochet work, and join it to ★ (between the 2nd and the 3rd beads of step 3) with a slip stitch.

6 Take 3 (gold) beads and close it with a chain stitch, then make 3 chain stitches.

7 Turn over the crochet work, and join it to ☆ (between the 19th and the 20th beads of step 4) with a slip stitch.

8 Take 20 (purple-red) beads and close it with a chain stitch, then make 3 chain stitches.

9 Turn over the crochet work, and join it to ★ (between the 2nd and 3rd beads of step 6) with a slip stitch.

10 Repeat steps 6. to 9. until the required length is reached.

11 2nd row: Make 3 chain stitches, and 1 single crochet in between the 1st and the 2nd beads of the 3 gold beads. Repeat to the end.

design-15

Triangular Hat

Beaded edging for a poncho

- Width of each motif: 2.3cm (7/8") • 10 motifs: Approx. 14.5cm (5 3/4")
- Size of edging - (194 motifs): Approx. 2.8m (9' 2 1/4")

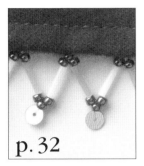

p.32

Material	Type/Product No.	Amount used		
		1 motif	10 motifs	Total
Yarn	DMC Cotton Perle #8/347 (red)	Approx. 8cm (3 1/8")	Approx. 80cm (31 1/2")	Approx. 18m (59' 5/8")
	Braided bead thread	Approx. 4cm (1 5/8")	Approx. 40cm (15 3/4")	Approx. 7.8m (25' 7 1/8")
Beads	Round, 8/0 (3.0mm), No.204 (gold)	3	30	582
	Round, 8/0 (3.0mm), No.125 (red)	3	30	582
	9mm-long bugle bead, No.1403 (white)	2	20	388
	Spangle, 5mm, No.16 (pink)	1	10	194
Needle	Crochet hook, No.8 (0.90mm); Beading needle	–	–	–

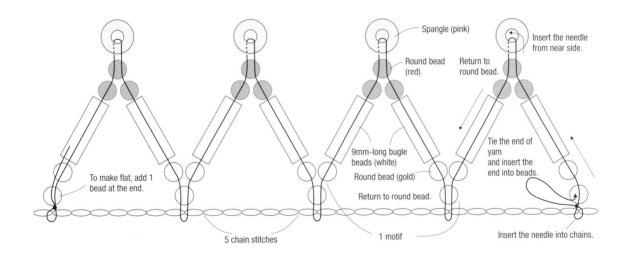

Spangle (pink)

Round bead (red)

Insert the needle from near side.

Return to round bead.

9mm-long bugle beads (white)

Round bead (gold)

Return to round bead.

Tie the end of yarn and insert the end into beads.

To make flat, add 1 bead at the end.

5 chain stitches

1 motif

Insert the needle into chains.

Chain stitches (upper side)

Insert the needle into 2 chain stitches, tie the end of yarn and insert the tail end into beads to hide it.

1 Make chain stitches with embroidery thread (Cotton Perle #8) until the required length is reached. Make extra chain stitches of 2 to 3cm (3/4 to 1 1/8").

2 Thread the beading needle with braided bead thread, then insert the needle into 2 chain stitches and tie a knot. Insert the thread tail into beads.

3 Thread the beads onto the bead thread as shown in the figure above, and insert the needle into 2 chain stitches again.

4 To make the crochet work flat, add 1 bead at the end and fasten it off. Insert the thread tail into beads. To ring the crochet work, return to the first bead and fasten it off. Finish the end in the same way.

design-16

Stars Twinkling over Snow

p.34

Beaded edging for a bag

• Width of each motif: 3.2cm (1 1/4")   • 10 motifs: Approx. 40cm (15 3/4")
• Size of edging - (16 motifs + 16 triangles): Approx. 94cm (37")

Material	Type/Product No.	Amount used		
		1 motif	10 motifs	Total
Yarn	DMC Cotton Perle #8/ECRU (natural undyed color)	Approx. 21cm (8 1/4")	Approx. 2.1m (6' 10 5/8")	Approx. 4.7m (15' 5")
	Braided bead thread	Approx. 34cm (13 3/8")	Approx. 3.4m (11' 1 7/8")	Approx. 5.8m (19' 3/8")
Beads	Round, 8/0 (3.0mm), No.103 (light brown)	36	360	673
	Pearl enamel bead, 3mm, No.304 (gold)	9	90	160
	Round, 8/0 (3.0mm), No.23 (aqua)	5	50	80
	6mm-long bugle bead, No.329 (bronze)	10	100	160
Needle	Crochet hook, No.8 (0.90mm); Beading needle	–	–	–

* Materials for the mobile case are not included.

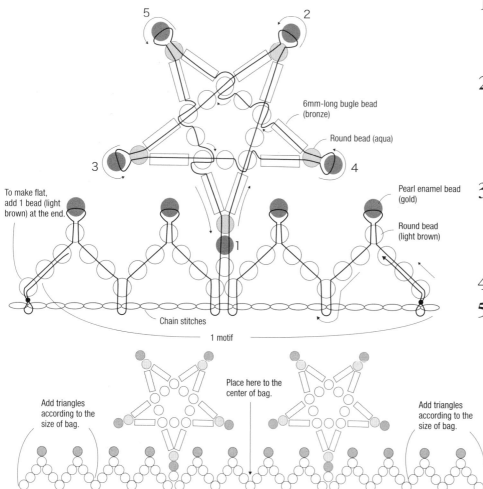

6mm-long bugle bead (bronze)

Round bead (aqua)

To make flat, add 1 bead (light brown) at the end.

Pearl enamel bead (gold)

Round bead (light brown)

Chain stitches

1 motif

Add triangles according to the size of bag.

Place here to the center of bag.

Add triangles according to the size of bag.

Chain stitches

1 Make chain stitches with embroidery thread (Cotton Perle #8) until the required length is reached. Make extra chain stitches of 2 to 3cm (3/4 to 1 1/8").

2 Thread the beading needle with braided bead thread, then join it to a chain stitch (see the diagram on p.77) at the end (insert the end of the braided bead thread into beads later). Thread the beads for 2 small triangles.

3 Make a star like an unicursal star. Thread the beads from 1 to 2, and fixing the tip of the star with a pearl enamel bead, continue in the order shown in the figure and return to 1.

4 Make 2 more triangles.

5 To make the crochet work flat, add 1 bead and fasten it off. Insert the end of the thread into beads. To ring the crochet work, return to the first bead and fasten it off. Finish the end in the same way.

Tips

For parts you cannot edge with beads, for example handles, cut off the thread or let chain stitches into invisible part.

Juicy Grapes

A wine-colored choker

- Width of each motif: 2.1cm (7/8")
- 10 motifs: Approx. 28.5cm (11 1/4")
- Size of edging - (12 motifs + 8 arches): Approx. 38cm (15")

p. 36

Material	Type/Product No.	Amount used		
		1 motif	10 motifs	Total
Yarn	DMC Cotton Perle #8/902 (purple-red)	Approx. 17.1cm (6 3/4")	Approx. 1.71m (5' 7 3/8")	Approx. 2.3m (7' 6 1/2")
	Braided bead thread	Approx. 20cm (7 7/8")	Approx. 2m (6' 6 3/4")	Approx. 2.6m (8' 6 3/8")
Beads	Round, 11/0 (2.2mm), No.332 (purple-red)	36	360	450
	Round, 11/0 (2.2mm), No.559 (gold)	9	90	116
	Treasure, small, 11/0 (1.8mm), No.A-421 (gold)	15	150	180
Needle	Crochet hook, No.8 (0.90mm); Beading needle	–	–	–

* Regarding the DMC Cotton Perle above, the length, including yarn for double crochet, is as follows: with 1 motif: 86cm (33-7/8"); with 10 motifs: 8.6m (28' 2-5/8"); in total: 11.6m (38' 3/4")

Bead threading order (○ shows new beads)

①→②→③→④→⑤→⑥→⑦→⑧→
⑨→⑩→⑪→8→7→⑫→5→⑬→
3→⑭→1 3→⑮→1 2→⑯→⑰→
⑱→15→⑲→14→⑳→19→㉑→㉒→
㉓→20→14→3→㉔→4→㉕→6→㉖→
㉗→㉘→25→㉙→24→㉚→29→㉛→㉜→
㉝→30→24→3→2→1

Antique bead (gold)

Small round bead (Purple-red)

Small round bead (gold)

Head of double crochet

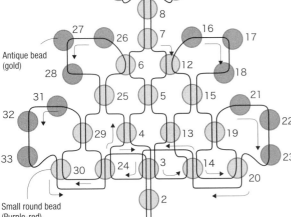

1 Make chain stitches with embroidery thread (Cotton Perle #8) until the required length is reached. Make extra chain stitches of 2 to 3cm (3/4 to 1-1/8").

2 Thread the beading needle with braided bead thread, then join it to a chain stitch at the end (see the diagram on p.77). Insert the end of the braided bead thread into beads later.

3 Thread the beads in the order shown in the figure to make 8 arches and a grape motif. 1 motif is completed when you make a grape stem.

1 motif

Tips

Make double crochets on chain stitches to make a tape. Put the beads picking the head of double crochet.

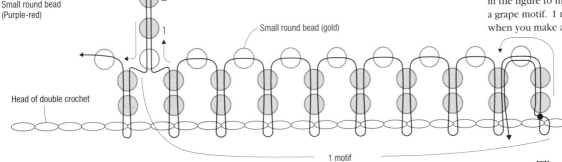

Add 8 arches to the end to make a symmetric pattern.

1 motif

8 arches

Put an attachment.

Put an attachment.

Chain stiches

Note: A motif consists of 1 grape and 8 arches. Adjust the length of the choker by making motifs necessary to fit your desired size.

p.38

Tiny Hot Peppers

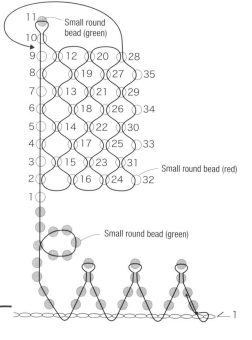

Beaded edging for kitchen items

- Width of each motif: 2.8cm (1 1/8")   • 10 motifs: Approx. 50cm (19 5/8")
- Size of edging - (6 motifs + 12 triangles): Approx. 36.5cm (14 3/8")

Material	Type/Product No.	Amount used		
		1 motif	10 motifs	Total
Yarn	DMC Cotton Perle #8/909 (green)	Approx. 29cm (11 3/8")	Approx. 2.9m (9' 6 1/8")	Approx. 2.5m (8' 2 3/8")
	Braided bead thread	Approx. 39cm (15 3/8")	Approx. 3.9m (12' 9 1/2")	Approx. 3m (9' 10 1/8")
Beads	Round, 11/0 (2.2mm), No.939 (green)	59	590	426
	Round, 11/0 (2.2mm), No.405 (red)	68	680	408
Needle	Crochet hook, No.8 (0.90mm), Beading needle	–	–	–

1 Make chain stitches with embroidery thread (Cotton Perle #8) until the required length is reached. Make extra chain stitches of 2 to 3cm (3/4 to 1 1/8").

2 Thread the beading needle with braided bead thread, then join it to a chain stitch at the end (see the diagram on p.77).

3 Thread the beads to make 3 triangles, 2 hot peppers and 3 triangles. Make a flat hot pepper with red beads first, and then connect the 28th and the 9th beads and continue as shown in the figure until you reach the 1st bead to roll the pepper into a cylinder.

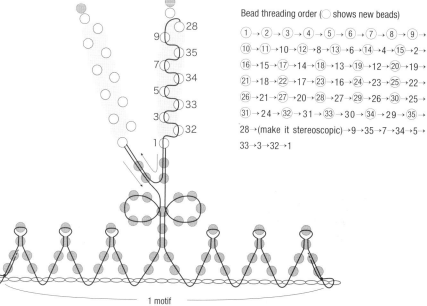

1 motif

Bead threading order (○ shows new beads)
①→②→③→④→⑤→⑥→⑦→⑧→⑨→
⑩→⑪→10→⑫→8→⑬→6→⑭→4→⑮→2→
⑯→15→⑰→14→⑱→13→⑲→12→⑳→19→
㉑→18→㉒→17→㉓→16→㉔→23→㉕→22→
㉖→21→㉗→20→㉘→27→㉙→26→㉚→25→
㉛→24→㉜→31→㉝→30→㉞→29→㉟→
28→(make it stereoscopic)→9→35→7→34→5→
33→3→32→1

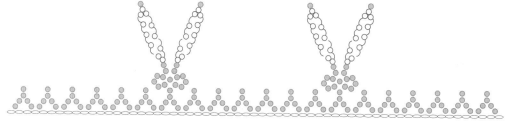

Tips
Make the same number of triangles at both ends according to the width of the kitchen cloth.

Adjust the length by making motifs necessary to fit to your desired size.

80

p. 40 | design-16 | Beaded edging for a scarf

- Size of scarf: Approx. 33 x 140cm (13" x 55 1/8")

- Size of edging (6 motifs): Approx. 33 cm (13") x 2 edgings

Material	Type/Product No.	Amount used	
		1 motif	12 motifs
Yarn	DMC S Dentelles #80 / 553 (purple)	68cm (26 3/4")	8.2m (26' 10 7/8")
	Special yarn for bead stitching	42cm (16 1/2")	5.1m (16' 8 3/4")
Beads	Round, 11/0 (2.2mm), No.907 (pink)	50	600
	Round, 11/0 (2.2mm), No.928 (purple)	28	336
	3mm-long bugle bead No.332 (purple-red)	10	120
	Round, 11/0 (2.2mm), No.557 (gold)	11	132
	3mm-long bugle bead No.22 F (gold)	10	120
	Round, 11/0 (2.2mm), No.332 (purple-red)	11	132
Needle	Crochet hook, No.8 (0.90mm); Beading needle		

* See page 78 for bead thread order.
A motif includes 2 stars in different colors.

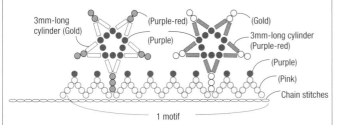

3mm-long cylinder (Gold)
(Purple-red)
(Gold)
(Purple)
3mm-long cylinder (Purple-red)
(Purple)
(Pink)
Chain stitches
1 motif

p. 43 | design-2&9 | Ring pillow

- Size of pillow: Approx. 14 (5 1/2") x 14cm (5 1/2")

- Size of edging (84 motifs): Approx. 56 cm (22")

Material	Type/Product No.	Amount used	
		1 motif	12 motifs
Yarn	DMC S Dentelles #80/B5200 (white)	10cm (3 7/8")	Approx. 8.4m (27' 6 3/4")
Beads	Round, 8/0 (3.0mm), No.33 (blue) — design-2	3	252
	Pearl, 2.5mm, No.200 (white) — design-2	1	84
	Round, 11/0 (2.2mm), No.33 (blue) design-9	90	
Needle	Crochet hook, No.10 (0.75mm)		

* For the crochet chart, see pages 62 and 65.

p. 43 | design-12 | Wedding pouch

- Size of pouch: Approx. 14 (diameter: 5 1/2") × 18cm (7 1/8")

- Size of edging (26 motifs): Approx. 44cm (17 3/8")

Material	Type/Product No.	Amount used	
		1 motif	12 motifs
Yarn	DMC S Dentelles #80/B5200 (white)	55cm (21 5/8")	Approx. 14.3m (26' 10 7/8")
Beads	Round, 8/0 (3.0mm), No.33 (blue)	18	468
Needle	Crochet hook, No.10 (0.75mm)		

* For the crochet chart, see page 74.

p. 42 | design-10 | Wedding veil

- Size of veil: Approx. 200 (6' 6 3/4") × 180cm (5' 10 7/8");
Circumference: Approx. 6.3m (20' 8")

- Size of edging (756 motifs): Approx. 6.3m (20'8")

Material	Type/Product No.	Amount used	
		1 motif	756 motifs
Yarn	DMC S Dentelles #80/B5200 (white)	17.5cm (6 7/8")	Approx. 132.5m (26' 10 7/8")
Beads	Round bead, No.33 (blue)	8	6,048
Needle	Crochet hook, No.10 (0.75mm)		

* For the crochet chart, see page 72.

1 Thread 2 bags of beads (680 beads/bag), crochet them, and then cut the thread after completing the last motif when finishing up with the beads.

2 Thread another 2 bags of beads and continue to crochet after connecting a thread to the last single crochet stitch at the end of the crocheted piece from step 1.

3 If crocheting the required length of the piece, secure the end of the yarn by threading on a bead.

Crochet with the new yarn.
New yarn
Thread beads.
Leave about 10cm (3 7/8") of yarn at each end for securing.

4 Sew approx. 3.5cm (1 3/8") wide lace onto the edge of the veil, by aligning the edges of both veil and lace, securing them with a running stitch and then whipstitching the ragged part of the lace.

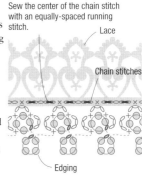

Sew the center of the chain stitch with an equally-spaced running stitch.
Lace
Chain stitches
Edging

5 Align the chains of edging with the edge of the lace and secure them with a running stitch. Fixing the right edges of both by pinning or with a clip on a board such as an ironing board will make this easier. Sew them carefully, pulling with an appropriate amount of tension.

Lace with the straight edge on the edging side and the ragged edge on the opposite side beautifully suit the curve of the veil.

p. 44 | design-10 | Christmas boots (small)

- Size of boots: Approx. 20 × 38cm (7 7/8" x 15")

- Size of edging (34 motifs): Approx. 32cm (12 5/8")

Material	Type/Product No.	Amount used	
		1 motif	34 motifs
Yarn	DMC Cebelia #30 / 816 (purple-red)	25cm (9 7/8")	Approx. 8.5m (26' 10 7/8")
Beads	Round, 8/0 (3.0mm), No.125 (red)	4	136
	Round, 8/0 (3.0mm), No.333 (green)	4	136
Needle	Crochet hook, No.10 (0.75mm)		

* For the crochet chart, see page 72.

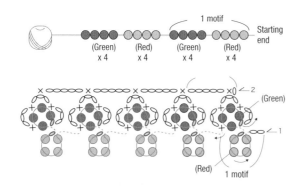

(Green) x 4 (Red) x 4 (Green) x 4 (Red) x 4 Starting end

(Green) (Red) 1 motif

p. 45 | design-15 | Ornaments:The Snowman & little bird

- Size of snowman: Approx. 7 × 12cm (2 3/4" x 4 3/4"); little bird:
  Approx. 12 × 8cm (4 3/4" x 3 1/8")

- Size of edging: snowman (14 motifs) Approx. 10cm (3 7/8"); little bird
  (12 motifs): Approx. 8cm (3 1/8")

Material	Type/Product No.	Amount used	
		1 motif	14 motifs
Yarn	DMC Cotton Perle #8/902, (purple-red)	4cm (1 5/8")	Approx. 56cm (22")
	Special yarn for bead stitch	2cm (3/4")	Approx. 30cm (11 3/4")
Beads	Round, 11/0 (2.2mm), No.103 (light brown)	2	28
	Round, 11/0 (2.2mm), No.908 (light pink)	4	56
	Spangle, 4mm, No.19 (white)	1	14
	3mm-long bugle bead, No.332 (purple-red)	2	28
Needle	Crochet hook, No.8 (0.90mm); Beading needle		

* For threading the beads, see page 77.

Make the edging of the garland in the same way.

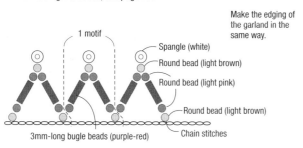

1 motif
Spangle (white)
Round bead (light brown)
Round bead (light pink)
Round bead (light brown)
3mm-long bugle beads (purple-red)
Chain stitches

p. 44 | design-3 | Christmas boots (large)

- Size of boots: Approx. 25 × 42cm (9' 7/8" x 16 1/2")

- Size of edging (20 motifs): Approx. 38cm (12 5/8")

Material	Type/Product No.	Amount used	
		1 motif	20 motifs
Yarn	Olympus Emmy Grande (pink)	60cm (23 5/8")	Approx. 12m (26' 10 7/8")
Beads	Bead pearl enamel gold, 3mm, No.304 (gold)	11	220
Needle	Crochet hook, No.6 (1.00mm)		

* For the crochet chart, see page 66.

p. 45 | design-16 | Garland (pink color)

- Size of garland: Approx. 6 (2 3/8") × 7.5cm (3")

- Size of edging (7 motifs): Approx. 18cm (7 1/8")

Material	Type/Product No.	Amount used	
		1 motif	7 motifs
Yarn	DMC Cotton Perle #8/902 (purple-red)	12cm (4 3/4")	Approx. 1.7m (5' 6 7/8")
	Special yarn for bead stitch	14cm (5 1/2")	1.2m (3' 11 1/4")
Beads	Round, 11/0 (2.2mm), No.103 (light brown)	22	154
	Round, 11/0 (2.2mm), No.332 (purple-red)	14	98
	Round, 11/0 (2.2mm), No.908 (light pink)	14	98
	3mm-long bugle bead No.22 (gold)	10	70
Needle	Crochet hook, No.8 (0.90mm); Beading needle		

* For threading the beads, see page 78.

Make the edging of the ornaments in the same way.

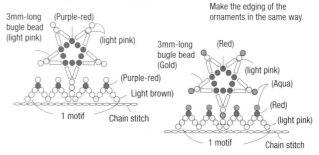

3mm-long bugle bead (light pink) (Purple-red) (light pink) (Purple-red) Light brown 1 motif Chain stitch

3mm-long bugle bead (Gold) (Red) (light pink) (Aqua) (Red) (light pink) 1 motif Chain stitch

p. 45 | design-16 | Garland (aqua colors)

- Size of garland: Approx. 6 x 7.5 cm (2 3/8" x 3")

- Size of edging (7 motifs): Approx. 18cm (7 1/8")

Material	Type/Product No.	Amount used	
		1 motif	7 motifs
Yarn	DMC Cotton Perle #8/902 (purple-red)	12cm (4 3/4")	Approx. 1.7m (5' 6 7/8")
	Special yarn for bead stitch	14cm (5 1/2")	1.2m (3' 11 1/4")
Beads	Round, 11/0 (2.2mm), No.908 (light pink)	27	189
	Round, 11/0 (2.2mm), No.125 (red)	14	98
	Round, 11/0 (2.2mm), No.143 (aqua)	9	63
	3mm-long bugle bead No.22 (gold)	10	70
Needle	Crochet hook, No.8 (0.90mm); Beading needle		

◆ : Appleton Crewel Wool (embroidery thread)

p. 46 | design-2 | Knit cap

- Size of cap (head circumference): Approx. 56cm (22")

- Size of edging (84 motifs): Approx. 67.5cm (26 5/8") × 2

Material	Type/Product No.	Amount used	
		1 motif	84 motifs
Yarn	◆ Appleton 695 (ocher)	1.1m (3' 7 1/4")	Approx. 92.5m (26' 10 7/8")
Beads	Wood bead, 3mm, α-128 (pink)	9	756
	Wood bead, 3mm, α-129 (dark pink)	9	756
	Wood bead, 3mm α-125 (red)	2	168
	Wood bead, 3mm, α-121 (brown)	2	168
	Wood bead, 3mm, α-160 (white)	2	168
Needle	Crochet hook, No.4 (1.25mm)		

* For the crochet chart, see page 65.

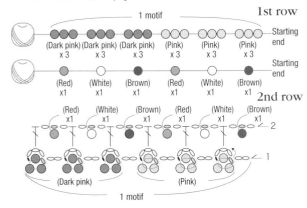

p. 47 | design-1 2 | Knit tote bag

- Size of bag (perimeter): Approx. 58cm (22 7/8")

- Size of edging (22 motifs): Approx. 58cm (22 7/8")

Material	Type/Product No.	Amount used	
		1 motif	22 motifs
Yarn	Very thin wool yarn (pink)	60cm (23 5/8")	Approx. 13.5m (44' 3 1/2")
Beads	Wood bead, 3mm, α-169 (turquoise blue)	2	44
	Wood bead, 3mm α-127 (yellow)	4	88
	Wood bead, 3mm α-121 (brown)	3	66
	Wood bead, 3mm α-120 (white)	9	198
Needle	Crochet hook, No.4 (1.25mm)		

* For the crochet chart, see page 74.

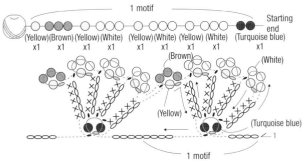

p. 47 | design-3 | Knit gloves

- Size of glove (wrist circumference): Approx. 19cm (7 1/2")

- Size of edging (2 motifs): Approx. 7cm (2 3/4") x 2

Material	Type/Product No.	Amount used	
		1 motif	84 motifs
Yarn	◆ Appleton 484 (blue)	1.24m (4' 7/8")	Approx. 5m (16' 4 7/8")
Beads	Wood bead, 3mm, α-121 (brown)	10	40
	Wood bead, 3mm, α-120 (white)	10	40
	Wood bead, 3mm, α-129 (dark pink)	2	6
Needle	Crochet hook, No.4 (1.25mm)	9	198

* For the crochet chart, see page 66.
Thread beads in reverse order for the left-hand glove.

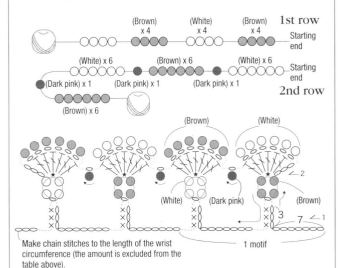

Make chain stitches to the length of the wrist circumference (the amount is excluded from the table above).

p. 52 | design-6 & 8 | Candle holder (D)

- Size of holder: Approx. 9cm x 140cm (3 1/2" x 55 1/8")

- Size of edging (11 motifs): Approx. 28cm (11")

Material	Type/Product No.	Amount used	
		1 motif	11 motifs
Yarn	DMC Cebelia #30/No.3865 (white)	1.5m (4' 11")	Approx. 16.5m (54' 1 5/8")
Beads	Small round bead, No.221 (browny gold)	41	451
Needle	Crochet hook, No.12 (0.75mm)		

* For the crochet chart, see page 71.

A. (design-14): For the crochet chart, see page 76. Use the same yarn and beads for the petit bag.

B. (design-17): For bead threading order, see page 79. Use the same yarn and beads for the choker. For this version, skip making a double crochet and attach beads to chain stitches.

C. (design-8): For the crochet chart, see page 71. Use DMC Cebelia #30 / No.816 for the yarn, and antique round beads, No. A-561 (green), No. A-557 (gold), No. A-553 (pink), No.A-917 (blue) and No.A-176 (silver) for the beads.

* Regarding yarn, the lengths shown under "Quantity" are for reference only. Allow 20 to 30cm (7 7/8 to 11 3/4") of yarn for the beginning and end of each row of crocheting.

p. 47 | design-10&7 | Decoration for boots

- Size of boot (perimeter): Approx. 32cm (12 5/8")

- Size of edging - 26 motifs: Approx. 33cm (13"); 2 motifs: Approx. 32cm (12 5/8")

Material		Type/Product No.	Amount used	
			1 motif	26 motifs
design-10	Yarn	◆ Appleton 947 (dark pink)	29cm (11 3/8")	Approx. 7.6m (24' 11 1/4")
	Beads	Wood bead, 3mm, α-160 (white)	4	104
		Wood bead, 3mm, α-166 (pink)	2	52
		Wood bead, 3mm, α-169 (turquoise blue)	1	26
		Wood bead, 3mm, α-161 (brown)	1	26
			1 motif	2 motif
design-7	Yarn	◆ Appleton 947 (dark pink)	1.4m (4' 7 1/8")	Approx. 4m (13' 1 1/2")
	Beads	Wood bead, 3mm, α-164 (green)	20	55
		Wood bead, 3mm, α-125 (red)	24	48
Needle		Crochet hook, No.4 (1.25mm)		

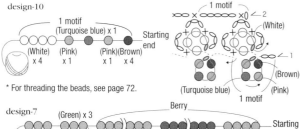

design-10

* For threading the beads, see page 72.

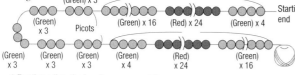

design-7

* For threading the beads, see page 70.
Make berries at both ends and control the length with chain stitches.
Make picots at desired positions on the chain.

p. 49 | design-1 | A linen parasol

- Size of parasol (length): Approx. 80cm (31 1/2")

- Size of edging (160 motifs): Approx. 2.52m (8' 3 1/4")

Material	Type/Product No.	Amount used	
		1 motif	160 motifs
Yarn	DMC S Dentelles #80/305 (moss green)	27cm (10 5/8")	Approx. 43.5m (142' 8 5/8")
Beads	6mm-long bugle bead, No.21 (silver)	2	320
	Round, 11/0 (2.2mm), No.241 (red)	5	800
Needle	Crochet hook, No.10 (0.75mm)		

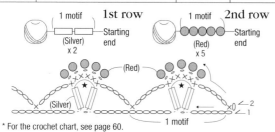

* For the crochet chart, see page 60.

p. 50 | design-5 | Coasters (purple/blue)

- Size of coaster: Approx. 12 × 12cm (4 3/4 x 4 3/4")

- Size of edging (butterfly x 1 + picot x 16): Approx. 48cm (18 7/8")

Material	Type/Product No.	Amount used	
		Purple	Blue
Yarn	DMC S Dentelles #80	397 (light purple): 3.7m (12' 1 5/8)	775 (aqua): 3.7m
Beads	Round, 11/0 (2.2mm), No.558 (silver)	8	8
	Round, 11/0 (2.2mm), No.265 (purple)	80	24
	Round, 11/0 (2.2mm), No.264 (blue)	24	16
	Round, 11/0 (2.2mm), No.932 (dark blue)		64
Needle	Crochet hook, No.10 (0.75mm)		

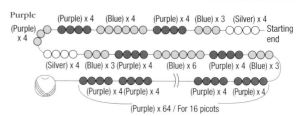

Purple

(Purple) x 64 / For 16 picots

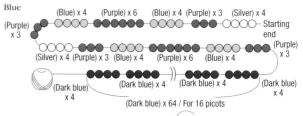

Blue

(Dark blue) x 64 / For 16 picots

* For the crochet chart, see page 68.

If 16 picots are completed, attach the edging around the coaster with a slip stitch. Control the length of edging by making chain stitches.

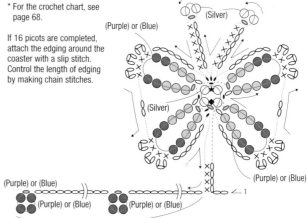

16 picots

An example of another application
Glass markers on p.50

Make a butterfly motif and then thread it onto a hook for earrings. Thread a Czech fire polish bead as an accent, and a motif is completed.
(Purple) α 6604-65 4mm (metallic fuchsia)
(Blue) α 6601-1 4mm (turquoise)

* DMC S Dentelles means DMC Special Dentelles.

p.53 | design-11, 8 & 10 | Box with 3 motifs

- Size of box: Approx. 9.5 × 9.5 × 4cm (3 3/4 x 3 3/4 x 1 5/8")
  [Size of cut-out window: Approx. 5.3cm (2 1/8") on each side]

- Size of edging (5 motifs): Approx. 4.5cm (1 3/4") x 3

	Material	Type/Product No.	Amount used	
			1 motif	5 motifs
design-11	Yarn	DMC S Dentelles #80 / 3778 (orange)	30.5cm (12")	Approx. 1.6m (5' 3")
	Beads	Treasure, small, 11/0 (1.8mm), No.A-554 (pink)	4	20
		Round, 11/0 (2.2mm), No. 557 (gold)	5	25
design-8	Yarn	DMC S Dentelles #80 / 3687 (dark pink)	33.5cm (13 1/4")	Approx. 1.7m (5' 6 7/8")
	Beads	Round, 11/0 (2.2mm), No.559 (gold)	7	35
design-10	Yarn	DMC S Dentelles #80 / 3778 (orange)	17.5cm (6 7/8")	Approx. 87.5cm (34 1/2")
	Beads	Treasure, small, 11/0 (1.8mm), No.A-560 (green)	4	24
		Round, 11/0 (2.2mm), No.551 (orange)	4	20
	Needle	Crochet hook, No.10 (0.75mm)		

* For the crochet chart, see page 73, 71 and 72.

design-11

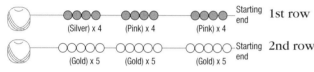

(Silver) x 4   (Pink) x 4   (Pink) x 4   Starting end   1st row

(Gold) x 5   (Gold) x 5   (Gold) x 5   Starting end   2nd row

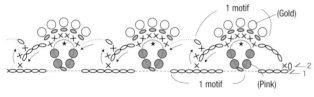

1 motif   (Gold)
1 motif   (Pink)

design-10

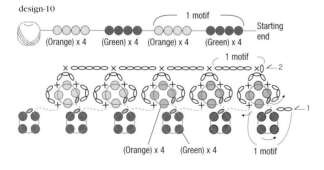

(Orange) x 4   (Green) x 4   (Orange) x 4   (Green) x 4   Starting end

1 motif

(Orange) x 4   (Green) x 4   1 motif

p.53 | design-8 | Card (large)

- Size of card: Approx. 12 × 16cm (4 3/4 x 6 1/4")

- Size of edging (16 motifs): Approx. 15.5cm (6 1/8")

Material	Type/Product No.	Amount used	
		1 motif	16 motifs
Yarn	DMC S Dentelles #80 / 3052 (moss green)	33.5cm (13 1/4")	Approx. 5.4m (17' 8 5/8")
Beads	Round, 11/0 (2.2mm), No.559 (gold)	7	112
Needle	Crochet hook, No.10 (0.75mm)		

* For the crochet chart, see page 71.

p.53 | design-17 | Small box with grape motif

- Size of box: Approx. 5.5 × 5.5 × 3cm (2 1/8 x 2 1/8 x 1 1/8")

- Size of edging (1 motif): Approx. 2.5cm (1")

Material	Type/Product No.	Amount used	
		1 motif	
Yarn	DMC Cotton Perle #8/917 (purple-red)	1.1m (3' 7 1/4")	
	Special yarn for bead stitch (purple)	20cm (7 7/8")	
Beads	Round, 11/0 (2.2mm), No.332 (purple-red)	38	
	Round, 11/0 (2.2mm), No.947 (green)	24	
Needle	Crochet hook, No.8 (0.90mm); Beading needle		

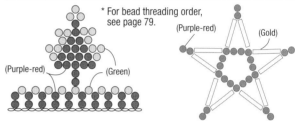

* For bead threading order, see page 79.

(Purple-red)   (Gold)

(Purple-red)   (Green)

p.53 | design-8&16 | Album

- Size of album: Approx. 17.5 × 11.5cm (6 7/8 x 4 1/2")

- Size of edging (10 motifs): Approx. 4.5cm (1 3/4") × 2

	Material	Type/Product No.	Amount used	
			1 motif	10 motif
design-8	Yarn	DMC S Dentelles #80 / 3687 (dark pink)	33.5cm (13 1/4")	3.35m (10' 11 7/8")
	Beads	Round, 11/0 (2.2mm), No.559 (gold)	7	70
design-16	Yarn	Special yarn for bead stitch	25cm (9 7/8")	
	Beads	Round, 11/0 (2.2mm), No.252 (purple-red)	25	
		9mm-long bugle bead, No.221 (gold)	10	
	Needle	Crochet hook, No.10 (0.75mm); Beading needle		

* For the crochet chart of design-8, see page 71.

p.53 | design-11 | Card (small)

- Size of card: Approx. 11 × 8cm (4 3/8 x 3 1/8")

- Size of edging (12 motifs): Approx. 11cm (4 3/8")

Material	Type/Product No.	Amount used	
		1 motif	12 motif
Yarn	DMC S Dentelles #80 / 917 (purple-red)	23cm (9")	Approx. 2.8m (9' 2 1/4")
Beads	Treasure, small, 11/0 (1.8mm), No.A-554 (pink)	4	48
	Round, 11/0 (2.2mm), No.21 (silver)	5	60
Needle	Crochet hook, No.10 (0.75mm)		

* For the crochet chart, see page 73.

(Pink) x 4   (Pink) x 4   (Pink) x 4   Starting end   1st row

(Silver) x 5   (Silver) x 5   (Silver) x 5   Starting end   2nd row

* Regarding yarn, the lengths shown under "Quantity" are for reference only. Allow 20 to 30cm (7 to 12") of yarn for the beginning and end of each row of crocheting.

- Size of piece: Approx. 42 × 16 cm (16 1/2" x 6 1/4") [Excluding the tape]

- Size of edging (400 motifs): Approx. 42 × 16cm (16 1/2" x 6 1/4")

Material	Type/Product No.	Amount used	
		1 motif	400 motifs
Yarn	DMC Cebelia #30 / 816 (purple-red)		95m (311' 8 1/8")
Beads	Round, 11/0 (2.2mm), No.51 (white)	72	1800
	Round, 11/0 (2.2mm), No.42D (orange)	6	150
	Round, 11/0 (2.2mm), No.55 (aqua)	6	150
	Round, 11/0 (2.2mm), No.44 (lime green)	6	150
	Round, 11/0 (2.2mm), No. 127 (light purple)	6	150
Needle	Crochet hook, No.10 (0.75mm)		

* Regarding yarn, the lengths shown under "Quantity" are for reference only.

* Allow 20 to 30cm (7 to 12") of yarn for the beginning and end of each row of crocheting.

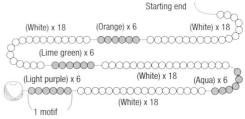

1 Thread beads onto yarn.
- 6 small round (seed) beads per motif.

Thread a set of beads in the following order as shown in the chart above: 6 light purple beads, 18 white beads, 6 aqua beads, 18 white beads, 6 lime green beads, 18 white beads, 6 orange beads and 18 white beads. Then thread 25 sets in total.

While 7 beads per motif are used for the base design (design-8), 6 beads per motif are used for this design in order to join the motifs in a well-aligned fashion.

2 Take 6 beads and then make the first motif based on the procedure for making the base motif on page 71.

3 When making the second motif, join the second loop of chain stitches with ★ of the first motif. When completing the third loop, take 6 beads and then close it for the next motif.

Make the loop of chain stitches on the right side of each bead loop from bottom to top first, then make the bead loop on the left side from top to bottom for each column.

Height: Approx. 15.5cm (6 1/8") [20 rows]

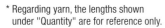

⑥
⑧ ⑤ ③
⑦ ④ ② ①

Approx. 42cm (16 1/2") [39 columns]

Attach chains to the tape [1cm (width) x 1m (length)] with slip stitches.

Make motifs in a vertical direction. For each column, make beads loops with the 3 loops of chain stitches on the right side from bottom to top first, then make the 3 loops of chain stitches on the left side of each bead loop from top to bottom.

4 Increase a motif for each column up to the 20th column, and then decrease a motif to the last column to work the piece into a triangular shape. Attach the chain stitches of the edge of the tape with slip stitches.

Tips

The overall impression created by each piece varies by the choice of color beads. Making test patterns before deciding on a finalized design is recommended. Enjoy creating a design unique to you.

◜ shows a chain stitch to close the loop with beads.

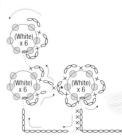

12 chain stitches

Chain x 8

The motif when finished crocheting.

Note: The middle part of this chart is omitted.

1 motif   The motif at the start of crocheting.

ABCs of Edging with Beads

Remaking your T-shirts, bags and various goods with bead edging is
entertaining and satisfying.

1 Measure the size of edging.

Once you've decided on the item to be used, measure the length of the part to be edged. Almost anything can be edged: the front placket or sleeve edge of a cardigan, the neckline of a blouse or T-shirt, the pockets or hems of jeans, stoles, camisoles and so on. After measuring the size, choose the edging design and prepare the materials needed. If 80cm (31-1/2") of edging is needed for a cardigan, divide the length by the length of 1 motif of the chosen design. For example, 1 motif of design-10 is 1cm (3/8"). Eighty divided by 1 is eighty, thus 80 motifs are needed. If 1 motif requires 8 beads, 8 x 80 motifs = 640 beads are needed. In addition, since the length of a knitted fabric may be different depending on the individual, prepare enough extra yarn and beads for 3 to 4 cm more than the calculated quantity as a safety margin. For example, in the above case, prepare an extra 24 to 32 beads in addition to the 640 beads for 80cm of edging.

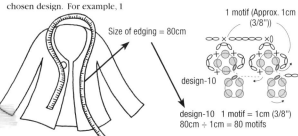

Size of edging = 80cm

1 motif (Approx. 1cm (3/8"))

design-10

design-10 1 motif = 1cm (3/8")
80cm ÷ 1cm = 80 motifs

2 Choose beads and yarn.

Once deciding on the item to be edged and the design, choose beads and yarn appropriate for the material and design. Lace yarn and small round beads work well with cotton fabrics such as T-shirt and jeans. Thicker lace yarn or embroidery thread and round beads are suitable for stoles and wool fabric. A combination of rough-hewn woolens and wood beads will create a folkloric taste. You can create a fine and delicate effect for the butterfly or rose motifs if using small round beads. Above all, the most important thing to consider is the combination of beads and yarn. Put together a test motif to find the best possible combination.

3 Create the edging with beads.

◆ When using the crochet hook

Thread the required number of beads, along with some extras [for 3 to 4cm (1-1/8" to 1-5/8")] onto the yarn. When using beads of two or more colors, be careful not to confuse the bead order. After threading the beads, crochet it a bit tightly according to the crochet chart. Take care that the shape and size of each motif is equal.

• When running short of yarn...

Add new yarn with beads at an indistinctive point, such as at the end of 1 motif. Do not tie the ends of both pieces of yarn because beads will not pass smoothly over the knot. Insert the end of a piece of yarn into chains or beads to make them less noticeable.

• When unwanted beads are mixed...

To simply take it off, break it with a nipper.

◆ When using a beading needle

Tighten the yarn each time you thread the beads to fix the shape.

• When running short of beads...

Allow 10cm (3-7/8") of yarn and cut it, threading beads on with a clew. Continue crocheting in the same manner as in cases when running short of yarn and hide the ends. You can also cut the required length of yarn and thread the beads from the end of that piece of yarn (the last end). In this case, pay attention to the order of beads (the reverse order to the first order).

4 Sewing the edging with beads.

Sew the finished edging with beads carefully to the edge of the fabric. You can sew it on a rim, on the upper side, or to the under side. Join the edging with beads a bit loosely using dress pins on fabric as a temporary measure, finally sewing it 3 chains apart.

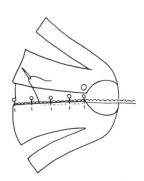

• Sewing appropriate for the material

Sew the edging on stretchy material such as knit with a blind stitch, allowing an extra margin of yarn. On the other hand, sew edging onto scarves with a running stitch to avoid sagging.

• Sewing on curved edges

Sew the edging along the curve with a blind stitch, allowing an extra margin of yarn.

• Sewing the edging on the upper side

Sew the edging on the upper side of the fabric with the same color yarn as that of the chain stitches.

Running stitch at every 3rd or 4th chain (Hook the part in between two chains.)

• Sewing the edging on the under side

Sew the edging on the under side of the fabric with a blind stitch with the same color yarn as the fabric.

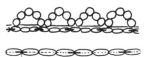

Blind stitch at every 3rd or 4th chain.

• Sewing the edging on a rim

Fit the edging on the rim of the fabric and join them with a blind stitch with the same color yarn as that of the chain stitches.

Blind stitch at every 3rd or 4th chain.

Authors

Midori Nishida

Ms. Midori Nishida is a professional craft artist whose work spans a variety of fields. Deeply moved and inspired by the "Turkish Embroideries and Oya Exhibition", she endeavored to create her own line of crafts and introduced Boncuk oya to Japan, adapting it into a more accessible form for Japanese crafters. The cultural exchange tour to Turkey in which she participated in 2006 turned her into a lifelong devotee of oya. She has since continued to study and perfect the art of "beaded edgings" with CRK design, co-author of this book, and has built a massive base of loyal fans both in and outside of Japan. In 2008, she appeared in "Oshare Koubou", an NHK TV craft show, which helped to make "beaded edgings" immensely popular in Japan.

C·R·K design

CRK design is a design firm made up of six graphic designers, Chiaki Kitaya, Kaoru Emoto, Kuma Imamura, Kumiko Yajima, Yasuko Endo, Noriko Yoshiue.
Their first craft magazine design project opened the door to their career in craft making and design. Today, they do everything from designing and production to book designing. In collaboration with Ms. Midori Nishida, co-author of this book, the group has generated an endless stream of creative ideas and designs for decorative edgings.
http://www.crk-design.com/

CRK design has held a number of "beaded edgings" exhibitions mainly in Tokyo and Kyoto, in addition to appearing on TV and sponsoring numerous workshops. They held a workshop at The 10th Nordic Knitting Symposium in July 2009, where the audience, made up of participants from Nordic countries, America and Asia, were swept away by the delicate beauty and charm of beaded edgings.

Profile of CRK design members

Chiaki Kitaya

Graduated from Musashino Art University Junior College of Art and Design. Through her planning and designing role at the Kazuko Endo Design Office, she discovered the joy of coordinating team efforts to create new and innovative products. This inspired her to establish CRK design in 1996.
She is currently in charge of creative and shooting direction, styling, graphic design and production management.

Kaoru Emoto

Graduated from Musashino Art University Junior College of Art and Design, and went on to study professional calligraphy in the U.S. Joined CRK design in 1996 as a founding member. She has designed numerous embroidery charts for craft magazines, and enjoys creating paper crafts applying her lettering & calligraphy skills.

Kuma Imamura

Graduated from Tama Art University. Started her home decor and craft design career at Kazuko Endo Design Office while still a student. Joined CRK design in 2001. She also does editing in addition to her primary role of graphic design. As a skilled knitter and crocheter, she is able to knit and crochet a wide range of items.

Kumiko Yajima

Upon graduating from Tama Art University, she embarked on a career as a mural and background painter, later joining CRK design in 2003. Her exposure to various materials and techniques awakened her interest in craft making. At CRK design, her main responsibilities include production and illustration.

Noriko Yoshiue

Worked for an ad agency as a graphic designer, and later went freelance. While designing craft-related publications, she has been creating patchwork quilts and lace crochet for a membership magazine. Enamored with the beauty of beaded edgings, she pours her heart and soul into her every creation. She is responsible for successfully creating motifs using thick yarn, something which has long been a challenge for crocheters.

Yasuko Endo

Upon graduating from the department of Apparel Design at Joshibi University of Art and Design Junior College, she joined the planning department of an apparel manufacturer, and later turned freelance. She is currently in charge of making craft and home décor products. Awakened to the beauty of Japanese kimono and vintage fabrics, she now takes lessons in Japanese dress-making techniques.

P.27 Y.Yura   P.45 T.Koizumi   P.33 Y.Ueki   P.56 K.Ishimoto   P.49 K.Yokoyama   P.21 MEU

Photographer

Yoshiharu Ohtaki

Graduated from the department of Photography at Kuwasawa Design School. Started freelancing after working as an assistant to a commercial photographer. Held the "Indian Time" exhibition (Nikon Salon) in 1985. Founded studio seek in 1997. He is a member of the Japan Photographers Society, and author of "A Journey into Japanese Textile Dyeing" (Graphic-sha Publishing Co., Ltd.)
http://www.seek-jp.com

Collaborators

Kanji Ishimoto, Chieko Ishimoto

Founded the Japan Turkey Culture Exchange Association in 1993. Is active in promoting person and cultural exchanges between Japan and Turkey to foster friendship between the two nations. Held "Turkish Embroideries and Oya Exhibition" in conjunction with the "2003: Turkey Year in Japan." Mr. and Mrs. Ishimoto are also members of the "Japan Year 2010 in Turkey" executive committee.

Creative collaborators for this book:

Yurie Yura

Is currently employed by the Kazuko Endo Design Office. Her collection of lacework and embroideries has been featured in a craft membership magazine on numerous occasions. Captivated by the dramatic collaboration of beads and lace, she actively promotes beaded edgings at the grass roots level.

Takako Koizumi

Graduated from Department of Oil Painting, Tama Art University. While creating and publishing block print pieces, she acquired an interest in craft making, and began making pottery, fancy crafts and leather crafts. She has participated in an annual picture book exhibition every autumn since 1996. She is the proud owner of a large collection of ornaments and fancy goods that are perfect for beaded edgings.

Yuko Ueki

As a shop assistant at a secondhand clothing shop in Harajuku, Tokyo, she set about designing reconstructed clothes and is now a successful designer of apparel, accessories and fancy goods. She currently devotes her time to creating and disseminating innovative ideas for clothing reconstruction.
http://www.uekiyuko.com

MEU

MEU has been an avid crafter since childhood. She is a skilled knitter and crocheter who excels at making things cute and sophisticated. She immersed herself in craft making during a seven-year stint in Belgium. After returning to Japan, she worked for a knit craft studio and a craft shop directly run by a Paris-based craft manufacturer. She is also involved in the handling of English yarn products.